The Book of Choice

Praise for
The Book of Choice

Powerful and transformational!

Much of our stored pain comes from the places and times in our life where we did not, or feel we did not, have a choice. It shouldn't surprise us then that much of our healing revolves around a reckoning with choice, with developing and harnessing a sense of deep agency. I know no better expert on this topic than Kim DeYoung and I know no better guide than *The Book of Choice*. I urge you to choose this book, in doing so you will be choosing yourself.

~Steph Jagger, Author of *Everything Left to Remember*

The Book of Choice is a game-changer!

This is more than a personal development book, it's the beginning of a movement! It literally has the power to help anyone reclaim and reframe life choices—past, present and future. Kim vulnerably shows us, through her own personal stories, how to apply these tools to change our relationships, choices and lives.

~Elena Deutsch, Founder/CEO of *WILL - Women Interested in Leaving Law*

Life-changing and thought-provoking.

The Book of Choice book holds the key to understanding not only your past, but how to better navigate the choices you'll make going forward. Kim is a master at introducing mapping, and her wisdom and insights will help you to better understand yourself. A must read!

~Kristine Newell, Author of *The Habit of Grateful*

An essential read.

The Book of Choice is a true masterpiece. It's an essential read for those who yearn for purpose and guidance in their lives. The captivating narratives have ignited a profound sense of inspiration and motivation within me, empowering me to take control of where my life is heading.

~Kathe Crawford, Author of *Unlocking Secrets: My Journey to an Open Heart*

THE BOOK OF
CHOICE

Kim DeYoung

NINTH HOUSE

PRESS

The Book of Choice: Mapping the Life You Want by Understanding the Life You Have

Copyright © 2023 by Kim DeYoung

Published in the United States by Ninth House Press.

Cover & interior design: Michelle Radomski

Paperback: 979-8-9877800-0-8

Ebook: 979-8-9877800-1-5

Library of Congress Cataloging-in-Publication Data

Names: DeYoung, Kim, author.

Title: The book of choice: mapping the life you want by understanding the life you have / Kim DeYoung

To my father who taught me how to navigate my choices on the pages of his legal pads.

Contents

Contents

Introduction

You have brains in your head.
You have feet in your shoes.
You can steer yourself in any direction you choose.
You're on your own.
And you know what you know.
And YOU are the one who'll decide where to go...
–Dr. Seuss, *Oh, the Places You'll Go!*

Mapping My Journey to What Is Possible

In late 2012, I received a compelling letter from a woman I'd worked with years earlier inviting me to attend an intimate coaching workshop. Her invitation's words filled my head with unspoken questions: Was her event another bright shiny object presenting itself to distract me? Was adding this expense to my growing, post-divorce credit card debt a smart decision? What did I hope to gain?

Each evening, for a period of days, I came back to her letter, reading the words that lingered in my thoughts:

Are you here for a higher purpose? Do you feel a sense of boredom and misalignment with your current situation? Do you feel a greater calling awaiting you?

Yes. Yes. And yes. Her questions resonated deeply yet I remained undecided about registering for the event.

Days later, still ambivalent about attending, an unexpected check for the precise amount of the workshop arrived in the mail—a payment from a client I'd forgotten was due.

The choice I'd contemplated but questioned was now an easy yes.

Driving to the workshop, my mother and I had yet another painful phone conversation. They always left me hurting deeply, wondering why it was so difficult to connect with her. That day, however, felt unlike any other. After a lifetime of challenging exchanges, that morning's was one too many and had taken an emotional toll I was no longer willing to endure.

While maneuvering the early morning roads on a windy Connecticut parkway, I made a choice that had lurked beneath the surface of my thoughts for some time: I decided to end my embattled relationship with my mother.

Arriving at the workshop minutes after our conversation, I felt tentative and fragile. No fancy makeup techniques could disguise my swollen eyes and I feared my internal noise would interfere with my ability to get what I wanted from the event. For a few minutes I sat quietly in my car, breathing deeply, hoping to compose myself and shake my negative energy before entering. Checked in, with my nametag in hand and not finding any familiar names among the others, I somberly took a chair at a table of strangers.

One by one, as the other participants presented their short introductions about why they were attending and what they hoped to gain from our two days together, my sense of dread grew. I felt in my core that mine was not going to be an ordinary business introduction, not after what had just happened.

The moderator eventually looked my way.

"Kim…," she said. "Tell us about you."

I stood slowly, scanned the room, and felt thirty sets of eyes staring at me. I prayed I would find a clear articulation of who I was and why I was there.

"Today I'm raw," I said, my voice trembling perceptibly. "On my drive to this event, I had an awful conversation with my mother and made a life-defining choice to end our relationship. And I'm left wondering, if I were more successful, more of everything, would she have loved me?"

Feeling exposed and vulnerable, I sat down as the room fell silent.

While the following moments felt surreal, I clearly recollect that as we took our morning break, hugs and warm words of solace abounded. Donna, a woman I'd not met before, held me tightly and whispered in my ear, "I've been where you are. You are my soul sister. You'll be fine."

Donna and I spent much of the next two days together, connecting about business and life. As the event drew to a close, she turned toward me, held my face tenderly in her hands, stared deeply into my eyes and said, "I need your brain and your brilliance to help me with a project. I'm hiring you."

I stared at her, wide-eyed and dumbfounded.

How, I wondered, in my state of utter fragility with my heart broken open, had she seen my goodness and my gifts? How did she know, with a confident inner sense, that I could help her with anything, let alone a business project? Donna, at that moment, was the angel I desperately needed, seeing more for me than I could for myself.

In the coming weeks, Donna and I developed an extraordinary working relationship—one that allowed me to show up at my best and share my professional and intuitive gifts so she could complete the project that mattered to her. When her project came to an end, the momentum begun by our work together continued. Similar consulting opportunities came my way, which led to new connections, which led to my hosting a virtual event.

While being interviewed to promote the event, words I was not aware of choosing streamed through me.

"As we make conscious choices and take deliberate actions, doors of possibility open."

These words, which were mine, but came from an unconscious place, continued to linger in my thoughts, demanding attention. I began to wonder what it would look like to explore the progression from making a choice, to taking inspired action, to then observing what unfolds and takes our lives in directions we could not have foreseen or imagined.

Prior to this experience, my perception of choice was pragmatic and cerebral. While I sensed the significance of my key choices, I didn't connect the dots and fully explore the ripple of each choice's repercussions. Some were big and consequential, others small and barely noteworthy. Some were choices I made consciously and intentionally; others were made nonchalantly with little thought for their ramifications.

I felt compelled to examine the layers of my simple but transformative choice to attend the workshop. If I'd chosen differently, I would not have encountered all the connections, opportunities and experiences that unfolded and led me to create an online coaching program, host a radio show and pursue the idea of writing a book.

Perhaps even more so, I felt compelled to look at the choice I'd made to end my relationship with my mother just before the workshop, which all but assured me I'd be showing up as my most authentic, raw self.

Being a visual thinker, I used a mind-mapping software to capture each of the clients, friends and opportunities that came into my life because of the choice to participate in the workshop. The map provided a concrete vehicle to document and make sense of seemingly unrelated ideas and experiences floating in my head, and facilitated me seeing how they were connected. My mapping tool enabled me to visually depict the complex web of thoughts and interactions around my choice simply and clearly.

Each branch of the map represented a new person or favorable circumstance I either created intentionally or that showed up miraculously. As the branches of my map grew and expanded, I could clearly see the effects and power of my one choice.

As I reviewed my map, I recognized two strikingly different vantage points.

When I focused on the right side of the page, which was the end of the map, and scanned left, back to the beginning, over all the branches that had transpired in a two-year period, I felt immense gratitude for all I brought into my life and that effortlessly showed up.

When I again focused on the right side where the branches ended, but this time looked to the right, into the distance, into the future yet to happen, I felt giddy with excitement about the possibility of what might fill that future space. The blank space seemed like the definition of untapped potential. *What choice could I make today that would lead to an entirely new map of opportunities and people that would come into my life tomorrow?*

Below is a zoomed-out image of the map for you to visualize these perspectives. The details are intentionally obscured—what's important for the moment is to see the big picture.

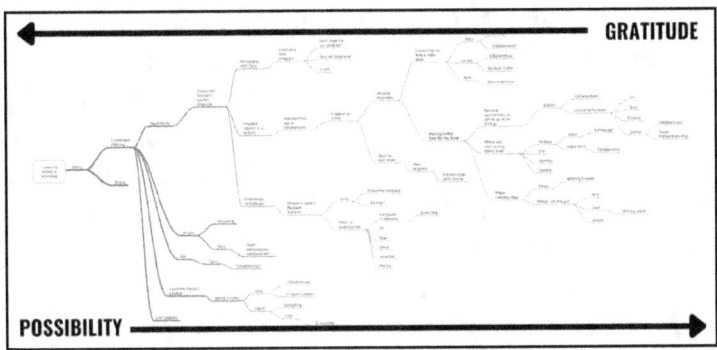

From the inception of my first map, I became hooked on the awareness I gained from my newly conceived process. I went back through years of past choices and created dozens and dozens of maps, all in a quest to gain awareness of my thoughts and actions. I mapped how my life unfolded because of distant choices, like choosing to add Art History to my college major and canceling a wedding two weeks before the day, to more recent choices like choosing to date a particular man, work with a new business partner, write this book, or say yes to opportunities I trust will bring me joy. Today, years after having developed this technique, mapping has become an integral tool to connect with and make sense of the varied and disparate segments of my life.

Showing my first map to my good friend Nancy, her eyes scanned the multitude of branches extending across the width of the page representing new clients and opportunities. She quickly grasped the magnitude of momentum and possibility inherent in making one choice.

Eager to be the first recipient of a map, Nancy and I explored her decision to join a high-end entrepreneurial coaching group. Why had she made this choice and what gave her the courage to do so? To make her choice, did she have to let go of any fears or limiting beliefs? What made her choice a pivotal one and how was she showing up differently? And, as a direct result of her choice, who had she met or what business opportunities had shown up?

After two hours of sifting through the complexity of her words and stories, I created a detailed map, replete with expanding branches, that captured the essence of her choice made many years ago. One branch focused on why she'd made the choice and why it had mattered to her. Another branch explored the shifts in her life that occurred because she made that decision.

Viewing the details of her choice from this new perspective enabled Nancy to see how a choice she'd made, which felt ordinary and could have moved beneath the radar of her consciousness, actually had greater importance and led to more than she'd previously realized.

As I shared my adventure of working with Nancy and creating her map with other close friends, they, too, wanted me to explore their choices and create maps for them.

And so what began as a relatively simple exercise of creating one map to trace the impact of one personal choice became a year-long journey exploring the various choices of twenty-nine fascinating people: friends I knew well, people I met serendipitously and special family members with whom I craved a deeper connection. With each person's choice and the safety and trust of our connection, we went on a deep-dive exploration to unearth what came into their lives from either a past choice they'd made or a present or future choice they were stepping into.

While I never sought to be a cartographer of my life, after making the decision to attend the workshop and the subsequent life-defining choice to end my relationship with my mother, I developed a unique process to look at how and why we make the choices we do.

The Examined Life

In the upcoming chapters, I'll introduce my mapping process and will walk you through the inner workings of many maps so you can gain insight into how to look at your choices with a fresh perspective. I'll present examples that illustrate the advantages of mapping and how they can be applied in a wide variety of scenarios, from personal challenges to relationship dilemmas to work issues. I'll share lessons across the breadth of my choices, as well as the decisions and rich stories of my clients, friends and family. You'll have the opportunity to benefit from our collective learning and determine how you can incorporate this level of inquiry and consciousness into your life.

Before diving into the whats, whys and hows of mapping, let me address the question at the heart of this book: **What is gained by looking at our choices with awareness?**

Imagine for a moment living a life without awareness—an unexamined life.

In that unexamined life, daily and weekly events transpire. In the absence of examination, you're relegated to coping and reacting to life's monotony, often victim to what's being doled out. With the unexamined life just happening, you lose touch with who you are and what you desire. Without pausing to reflect upon your choices, you walk blindly through life unaware of the potential you possess, oblivious to the limitations you unwittingly place upon yourself.

When you shift your attention to living an intentional and examined life, it comes alive through awareness.

In this examined life, you're choosing thoughtfully and acting consciously. By purposefully drawing insights from past choices, you're shaping the future you want. As you acknowledge that parts of your life are not in alignment with what matters to you, you can choose to either accept those parts as they are, or actively change them. You can shift what is out of sync with your true self to what you want it to be by making a new choice.

Making choices with intention allows you to acknowledge what you value and put it into action. With each new choice, you have an opportunity to take a stand for yourself and choose how you'll respond to what's showing up in your path. As you find your way, removing layers of what doesn't serve you to uncover what does, making informed choices at each crossroads allows you to assess if you're moving closer to what you want.

Consciously reflecting on your choices empowers you to live an examined life, to cultivate awareness and to take charge of where your life is heading. As you engage with your choices, the mapping process encourages you to ask thought-provoking questions, to listen intently and compassionately to your answers and to foster contemplation.

The deeper you move into the book, you'll see through examples how looking at your choices is transformative. By understanding the life you have, you can more thoughtfully move toward the life you want.

The choices and stories captured represent a wide range of ages and stages. Choosing is a universal experience relevant to every demographic. Regardless of your age and stage, imagine, as you read each story, that you're the one navigating the choice presented. Try on each circumstance considering how you might have answered the questions at both a younger age and how you'd answer them with today's wisdom.

Throughout the upcoming chapters, I'll share visuals of numerous maps plus a range of questions you can use to unearth relevant details about your choices.

For easy reference, I've created a resource page, (http://kimdeyoung.com/ChoiceResources) where you can access templates for different types of maps and map questions in one place, as well as videos of the map-making process.

To get the most value from the book, I suggest reading it once without making any personal maps. Take your time absorbing the ideas without feeling compelled to apply them immediately. Once you've familiarized yourself with the mapping language and the building blocks of maps, let the reality of where you are in your life guide you to the section of the book that will benefit you most.

- If you're considering ending a relationship and want suggested questions to reflect upon, move to Part 3 about Present Choices.

- If you're struggling with consequences related to a past choice you've made, go to Part 4 about Past Choices.

- If you're contemplating a future choice wondering what's possible, read Part 5 about Future Choices.

The book is organized in a thoughtful manner allowing you to return and see in which element of your life you need the most support.

Let this book and the tools within be a treasured guide and resource for you to return to at key junctures, supporting you to make your meaningful choices with intention. Let the questions in this book open you to creating a dynamic internal dialogue with yourself. Let this book be a precious gift you share with your friends, family and children as they seek to bring a greater level of thought and consciousness to their choices.

I wish you love and joy as you embark on this powerful journey of discovery and trust that great insights await you. If you'd like my support for anything you're navigating, please connect with me via my website http://kimdeyoung.com/ChoiceResources.

Author's Note: All names and other defining characteristics have been adjusted in order to protect the people who traveled with me on this journey. Any resemblance to actual people is purely coincidental. When personal maps are shared, their details are blurred, their content is changed to generic terms, and they are intentionally shown from an aerial view to protect private details.

PART 1

Your Choices Are Your Teacher

It is our choices, Harry, that show what we truly are,
far more than our abilities.

–J.K. Rowling, *Harry Potter and the Chamber of Secrets*

CHAPTER 1

Choice Mapping
The What and the Why

A map is a visual representation of a singular choice you made, a choice you are making or a choice you will make. A map is a vehicle to take all the details you can derive from a choice and organize them simply so the insights you gather are easily accessible for your review.

Since creating this process, I've been using mapping as a tool to live an examined life, turning to it when I want to flesh out and make sense of a gamut of thoughts, or look at puzzling situations through a lens of expansive curiosity.

Maps are a powerful tool allowing you to become your own guide, a self-discovery method helping you find your way from where you are to where you want to go.

As you experiment with the practice of mapping, you'll frequently ask these questions:

- What has happened because I made this choice?
- What will happen when I make this choice?

The mapping process allows you to draw yourself out by asking questions and paying attention to the first answer that presents itself. As you capture your answers in bite-sized nuggets you'll continue probing with the next intuitive or logical question, listening for a succinct answer. In the following chapters, I'll provide you with more targeted questions to serve as a jumping off point to build your maps, and more deeply explore your choices.

Mapping gives you the opportunity to stop, reflect and move forward with greater cognizance. As you pay attention to the details of your choices, the perspective with which you view your life will become richer and more expansive as you notice and foster consciousness about the journey your decisions are creating.

Mapping supports you to get clarity around your choices, and guides you through the confusion that surfaces when you become mired in your choice's details. So often big choices feel overwhelming. Mapping creates a tangible framework to organize the details of the difficult decision, providing structure to even the most complicated choices, making a challenging decision feel more manageable.

Over the years I've been using maps to guide myself as well as coaching people to guide themselves by creating maps of their own. The mapping process extracts the intricacies, nuances and key reflections around the complexity of your choices and distills them into tangible, salient points you can visually grasp and interpret.

The act of creating a map urges you to stop and contemplate your choice in greater depth. By translating multifaceted emotions and experiences into clear, digestible words which populate your map, you have the potential to better understand yourself and what you're navigating.

Mapping is an opportunity to gain insight and self-awareness as it aids you in being more present. As you practice mapping, your sensitivity to the nuances of your choices will increase. You will see clearly how each choice has led you to where you are today, and you'll bring greater mindfulness to making your future choices.

How Mapping is Different from Journaling

Mapping is distinct from journaling. In journaling, your words, thoughts and feelings flow fluidly onto a page. Key turning points are often obscured in the myriad of details within narrative journal format causing you to lose sight of what's truly significant.

The goal of mapping is not to free-write as you would in your journal, but to engage in a dialogue with yourself, asking incisive questions and capturing the answers as short truthful statements. The brevity of the format encourages you to hone your words into gems that resonate as your truth. Your questions and corresponding answers will form the foundation for your map.

When I began writing this book, I feared the specifics of mapping might be overwhelming for those not technically inclined. What I've come to understand is that the actual process of how you document your choices is secondary to what you discover as you immerse yourself in the inquiry and exploration of why you made or will make a choice. More important than what your map looks like is the process you undertake to uncover your truth.

As you reflect upon the decisions you've made in your past and visualize those you'll make in your present and future, you create an opportunity to impact your relationships, your career path and your confidence. Expansively considering your choices allows you to venture into a profoundly personal and spiritual journey, noticing the richness of the terrain you've traveled, seeing where you've been stuck, while recognizing untapped paths of potential.

The inquiry process, which I'll guide you through, supports you to flesh out the components of your choice and continue asking yourself questions that enable you to go deeper, accumulate more details, gather more insights and learn more about yourself—who you were, who you are, who you will be—so that you can use this information to make more thoughtful choices going forward.

Mapping is a tool for exploration that is always available to you, and gives you an accessible process for approaching big issues. Asking curious, pointed questions as you pull back layer upon layer of your truth allows you to comprehend all that's happening and discern what may be keeping you stuck.

During the journey of exploring my choices, there have been times I've actively mapped, and times I've lost sight that I have access to this tool. When I inevitably reach for this trusted companion, I'm astounded at the clarity I feel.

Giving greater attention to your choices is a practice you have the opportunity to embark upon daily. Should you find that you fall out of the habit of examining your life, as you may with any healthy discipline you've cultivated, you can carve out quiet time to resume it again. It's as simple as that.

As you move through the book, you'll use the maps and accompanying questions to support you in the following ways:

- How to view your past choices with compassion and forgiveness.

- How to reflect upon your past stories with a fresh and objective perspective.

- How to engage in the inquiry and exploration of why you made or will make a choice.

- How to coach yourself through choices you're making in the present to ensure you're heading in a direction that matters to you.

CHAPTER 2

What Choices Reveal

Every day you make choices—some big, some small—but particular choices are deeply meaningful because they demonstrate *who you are, what you value, where you've been and where you're going.*

Looking back and exploring what emerged from a choice you made gives you permission to take 100% ownership of it and any subsequent actions.

Certain intentional, proactive choices will stand out clearly in your mind; these are the BIG ONES—the ones you can easily recount—whether you married, what you chose to study in college, what job you took, where you moved, whether or not you chose to have kids. Then there are your smaller, seemingly less life-altering choices, often not on your radar, such as: choosing to attend a workshop, accepting an invitation or deciding to begin a yoga practice, that may require delving deeper into the recesses of your thoughts to excavate and uncover. Often, it's only upon reflection, as you retrace your steps and look for connections, that you can appreciate the great impact a small choice had in your life.

It's possible you've spent countless hours ruminating upon whether your big choices were right or wrong and how their consequences affected you along the way. You may wonder what could have been had you chosen a different path, causing you to feel self-doubt. It's natural when thinking about past choices to focus on a simple binary question: Was that choice good or bad? This type of thinking is tied to judgment, shame and doubt, and distracts you from the abundant information that is concealed within each choice.

There's more to gain by approaching choice from a place of deeper exploration and inquiry—seeking to understand what your choices can teach you about yourself.

Becoming an investigator of your life, excavating your past for answers and clues, lets you view yourself with kinder, more soul-seeking eyes. When perched on your own shoulder as an observer, you create emotional distance. This space enables you to sit with your questions and allow your answers to present themselves. During this process, you don't need a plan of action for what you'll uncover—keep asking, keep listening, allowing your answers to flow without any attachment or worry as to what you'll do with them. Trust that as you gather the answers to your challenging questions you can handle whatever arises.

During my first mapping year, I was profoundly introspective and reflective. I carefully examined my past in an attempt to understand what truly motivated me, what got in my way, what mattered to me, and how I wanted to show up as I moved into the next phase of my life. Acting as my own coach, I used guiding questions to dissect my key choices so I could better understand who I was and how I'd gotten to this place in my life.

- What motivated me to make that choice?
- Why did I choose that option when others were pushing me in a different direction?
- Did I listen to my intuition or ignore it?
- How did I show up at the time?
- Did I make my choice to please someone else?
- What did I hope would happen?
- Did I make the choice on my own or with support?
- What became possible because of that choice?
- How did I shift after the choice?

In asking these questions, I sought to understand details about my past thoughts and actions. I used my new tools of inquiry and mapping, plus my deep desire for answers, to explore the lessons I'd learned in making my key choices. Putting my life under deep scrutiny allowed me to see all that can be revealed through sustained inquiry. With continued practice, I honed this process and now share it so you can apply it to your life in the way that best suits you.

Over a decade ago, I began inviting groups of women to meet at my home based on one singular criterion—they each made me happy. Connection is my highest value, and bringing great women together brings joy into my life. At one of these gatherings, with choice very much on my mind (as it often is), I asked everyone to indulge me by sharing five key choices that define who they are and how those choices set the foundation upon which they're proud to stand.

Some of the women I knew well, others were new to my circle, but hearing the details of each woman's choices forged an immediate sense of deeper connection. No matter how different our backgrounds and stories, or how painful our choices may have been, we felt the humanity of each story, and appreciated a sense of deep solidarity as each woman spoke her truth.

A handful of the women made a meaningful decision related to being a parent. At twenty-two, one woman chose to have her boyfriend's baby against her parent's wishes, knowing she'd be disowned. A married woman with one child consciously chose not to have a second baby, a decision that bucked the desires of her close friends and family. A fifty-year-old grandmother, educated at an all-girls Catholic school, chose not to have an abortion at sixteen and insisted she get tutored, allowing her to graduate top in her high school class.

Many of the women walked away from corporate and supposedly stable professions to write a book, learn new skills, launch a start-up or pursue an entrepreneurial venture. They chose to leave relationships, take a stand for themselves and be alone rather than settling. Many shared personal stories that involved taking a leap to relocate to a new city, having an intuitive sense they needed a move to shake up their lives.

While there was great disparity in the choices the women shared, there were also striking commonalities: a deep inner strength, a courageous desire to take meaningful risks and a willingness to make big life changes even when it contradicted other people's wishes for them.

You have a choice in how you reflect upon the past. You can look back from a place of judgment, assessing what you did wrong and beating yourself up for all you wish you'd done differently, or you can mine your past for your key choices, made in a moment of strength, that set the tone and inform who you are today. These choices will stand out as lighthouses, each guiding the way to the next.

While there's certainly a place for, and a benefit to, looking at your dark spots, those parts you might wish to keep hidden, in the upcoming chapters we'll focus on examining your past choices to see how they tell a story of strength that informs who you are. Then, later on, we'll delve deeply into how to recover from any shame or guilt you may feel over perceived bad choices.

Five Intentional Choices

I invite you to take yourself on a journey. Look back over your life to **identify and focus on five intentional choices** that led you to where you are. As you begin, you may find this process challenging because your life has been full of choices. How do you sift through the multitude of decisions to determine the important ones that best illuminate who you are?

Let me demonstrate how I walked two clients through their pasts, supporting them to determine their five choices so you can get the gist of how to apply this exercise to yourself. Then I'll invite you to witness examples of a more involved exploration process. Equipped with both options, you can choose how deeply you'd like to go and how closely you want to examine your life.

During an intimate workshop I hosted, I encouraged eleven women to reflect upon lessons they learned from past choices and examine stories they'd created about themselves because of those choices. I guided them through an exercise to gain clarity on their significant choices and then assisted them as they narrowed those down to the ones that were most informative about who they are today.

As we began the exercise, my client Becca said, "Kim, I'm confused, I've made so many choices in my life, how do I choose the ones that are most meaningful?"

"Focus on the substantial ones you consciously made," I advised. "The ones that were intentional, the ones you had a reason for making. Don't focus on the ones you made without awareness."

The first choice Becca recounted was going to college because she had to prove something to herself. As the "pretty sister", she wasn't raised to believe she was smart and had to work diligently to get high grades and graduate magna cum laude.

Her next meaningful choice was to start her first wellness business because she craved independence and dreamt of making a difference. Her third choice was to move away from the pace of New York City to the rural and bucolic environment of upstate New York. Her next choice was to take all she'd learned over the years to become a coach and help others.

Years later, Becca became ill, and in spite of her medical knowledge, wasn't getting the information and support she needed to heal. She felt despondent and frustrated. Wanting to help others avoid what she'd experienced, she made her fifth major choice to return to her medical and wellness roots.

After Becca completed the exercise, I invited Julia to share her five choices.

"In college, I made the choice to take an art course. It was more fun than my other options and it paved the way for my becoming an artist."

"What about your next choice?" I questioned.

"I needed to find my voice and chose to enter a 12-step recovery program."

For her third choice, having always been a caregiver, making everyone in her family the food they wanted, Julia chose to stop serving them and focus on her own health by eating a macrobiotic diet. If her family wanted to eat what she was eating, great, if not, they could cook for themselves.

"What was your fourth choice?" I inquired.

"Needing to take care of myself, I chose to get divorced. Going macrobiotic had set me on a path of not being a caregiver."

"And your final choice?"

"Excited to experience other people and their cultures, I chose to take a year-long expedition around the world. Having the time, space and money, I wanted adventure and was ready to embark on something completely out of the box."

When Becca and Julia made their choices they weren't necessarily looking ahead to the future, but were taking a stand for something that had meaning for them in the moment. Each observed that her choices had far-reaching repercussions and provided information about what she values, and how she became who she is today.

Determining Your Five Key Choices

There are two components to exploring your key intentional choices.

1. First, gather your choices.
2. Second, investigate them through greater inquiry.

Selecting your key choices is not a scientific or highly mentalized process—it's simply a matter of tuning into a choice you remember making consciously that feels meaningful, and then following the path from one choice to the next. These choices are pillars from which you can move into deeper exploration.

My advice is to consider only those choices you made consciously and that you perceive without judgment. See yourself at your younger age weighing the options you pondered as you made your choice. View yourself with kindness and empathy, knowing you made the best choice based on who you were at the time. This exercise allows you to recollect your past, without regret, from a place of strength and empowerment, acknowledging that certain choices brought you to where you are today. These are the choices that define who you are and what you stand for.

Before moving into examples of deeper exploration, which I'll explain in the following chapter, let me guide you through an exercise so you can determine your key choices.

Grab your journal or laptop and light a candle. Close your eyes, get quiet and breathe deeply. Take yourself back in time to a younger version of yourself, recollecting the first choice you made intentionally, one that truly mattered to you. This may have been in your teens or twenties. Skim through your memory's archives seeing yourself at different stages and in varied environments. Continue moving through the years, recalling more. Let your list grow, enjoying the process. Pause at meaningful intervals to reminisce about who you were and what you were navigating. Concentrate on building your list. Take your time, and do not worry if your list is long or short.

Consider these examples as a springboard to begin your reflection.

- I chose to attend a particular school
- I chose to embark upon or end a relationship
- I chose to start or leave a job
- I chose to move
- I chose to take a trip
- I chose to get married, or not
- I chose to do something others didn't want me to do
- I chose to have or not have children
- I chose to hire a coach or therapist
- I chose to do something that scared me
- I chose to do something fun
- I chose to ask for what I want
- I chose to take a class
- I chose to write a book
- I chose to sing with a band
- I chose to learn a new skill

As you review your list, note only the choices you made consciously, ones where you may have experienced challenging moments of indecision. Choose the five that you feel had the greatest impact on who you are today.

If you have a shorter number of years to draw from, your list of total choices will likely be fewer and may have a similar flavor to those of your peers: the choice to attend a particular college, to study abroad, to end a relationship, to move out of your parents' home or to take a particular job.

If you have a broad life's vista, your list may be long. Choose the five that feel most resonant and impactful for you now. This thought-provoking exercise allows you to look at your life and who you are from a new perspective. Should you repeat this exercise at five and ten-year intervals, you may notice shifts in your five choices, one receding in importance as another takes its place.

CHAPTER 3

Clarity and Impact of Your Big Five

Once you decide which choices stand as the pillars in your life, the next step is to explore each one with greater inquiry. When you identify the strengths that allowed you to make those choices, you can call upon this fortitude to support you in navigating new choices you're making today.

In the following examples, I share my personal experience with how I reflected on five key choices that have charted my life's path to date. Narrowing down fifty years of choices to an integral few allowed me to establish connections between seemingly unrelated parts of my life. Each of my choices led to the next intersection, revealing previously veiled information about my guiding values.

Once I identified my most significant choices, I took myself back in time to observe myself navigating the crossroads of each decision. Who was I at that time? How was I showing up and what did I hope would happen because of each choice?

With a wiser, compassionate perspective, I recognize I made the best choice at that time using what was available to me. I observe that what may have appeared to be a short-term choice because it felt right in the moment had greater significance in the unfolding of my life.

As you begin your own examination, use these two questions to dig deeper into each conscious choice you made:

1. How did you feel at the time you made each choice? (Note: If you can't recall how you felt, ask yourself how you feel about that choice now.)

2. What positive qualities did you demonstrate in making your choice that you can now embrace and claim?

Intentional Choice #1 — Adding Art History to My College Major

I made my first meaningful choice in college when I chose to expand my major from Economics to include Art History.

At the time, it was a choice that didn't have great magnitude. I didn't love Economics, wanted to give myself a broad college education and take something more fun. Art History beckoned. Simple. I was twenty years old and it was a short-term choice that felt right in the moment. I gave my long-term future little thought and didn't foresee how that one choice, which seemed minor, would drastically affect the path I took, the trajectory of my life, and where I was led.

I recall the sensation of uncertainty as my inner critic judgmentally asked if I was making a serious mistake that would affect me professionally. Would I ever find a job to support myself? Was I completely arrogant thinking I knew what was right for me?

While these niggling doubts echoed loudly in the quiet spaces of my thoughts, I knew deep in my gut I'd made the right decision.

When I look at this choice from where I stand now, I see how a decision made at twenty has informed the entire path of my life. With this choice, I found my way into my own definition of visual creativity, which had been my mom's fiercely guarded domain. She was the official artist of our home, painting with geometric perfection. I often felt chastised for being messy and coloring outside the lines—a metaphor which trailed me much of my adult life. Choosing Art History, while I didn't know it at the time, was my first step on a journey to own my creativity, which had different qualities than my mother's.

In this choice I also see the growing presence of my inner strength, even in the face of fear. My father, an extremely strong influence in my life, approved of Economics as my major believing I had great potential to be involved in business. How would he respond when his perfect child, who had always listened to him, done well and followed his lead, told him she was breaking free? Would he lash out? Would I be able to hold my ground?

While I recall my trepidation preparing to share my choice with him, my twenty-year-old self had a moxie that didn't allow fear to permeate my decision. In declaring my independence, I demonstrated to myself that regardless of what others might choose for me, I am the final authority on what I believe is in my best interest.

Intentional Choice #2 – Moving to San Francisco

My next meaningful choice occurred at twenty-five when I chose to leave New York City and move to San Francisco to take a job with The Gap.

The Gap began reaching out to me at the start of my career, but the timing was never right for me to consider the cross-country move. When they approached me after an emotionally taxing day at work, I was open, and after receiving their compelling offer I said yes without consulting anyone. I quit my job, left my college boyfriend who I'd been living with in the city, and packed up to move across the country. It was a gut-based decision that felt completely right. I knew if we were going to work, I had to take care of myself and trust that our relationship could weather me taking charge of my own life and forging my own path.

Moving to San Francisco set the foundation for me being someone who makes decisions for myself, uses my intuition without consultation and trusts that the choices I make in the moment will serve me later on.

Intentional Choice #3 – Canceling My Wedding

My third major choice, at age twenty-seven, was to cancel the wedding with my college boyfriend—two weeks before the wedding date. We'd had a tumultuous engagement. He was coping with his dad's recent murder, we lived on opposite coasts, my mother was organizing the wedding, and we had no post-wedding plans for when we'd live in the same location.

Shortly before the wedding date I received a call from the rabbi who was going to perform our ceremony. "Kim, I've never made a call like this, but when we met weeks ago, and you sobbed deeply about your pain and the stress of the past year, I felt the need to call you so you could address the question of whether you're making the right decision to marry."

His words hit me hard. They contained a raw truthfulness I was only able to hear from a stranger, a man I'd known for scarcely an hour.

After returning home to San Francisco from our pre-wedding meeting in New York, I felt heavy-hearted. The first wedding gift had arrived and was awkwardly sitting on my living room floor. I forced myself to open the box to discover dishes from his aunt that carried the weight of a gift I did not want. Even though I hadn't officially decided what to do, I was reluctant to throw the box away already knowing intuitively I'd be returning the dishes. I knew the choice I needed to make yet I questioned, in light of his father's recent murder, could I do another thing to him that was out of his control?

I called my father.

"I know you've put money down for deposits and we have relatives coming in from out of town, but how would you feel if I canceled my wedding?"

And in the kindest words, which still warm my heart and bring tears to my eyes, he said, "Kim, do what you need to do, none of that matters in the big picture of your life."

And so, I made the dreaded phone call, canceled our wedding and ended a nine-year relationship. I knew it was better to be single than to stay in a relationship that wasn't right for me. People at work thought I was brave, but bravery never crossed my mind. My motivation was to take care of myself and acknowledge, with honesty, that I had not been thriving.

I sat with the uncertainty of whether I'd be forever single, and the remorse of realizing my choice would hurt a man I deeply cared about. While my feelings were uncomfortable, I chose to not let them get in the way of making a decision I knew had to be made.

At twenty-seven, while I couldn't foresee what this choice meant for my future, I knew deep in my gut this pivotal decision would change the course of my life. Canceling our wedding not only freed me from that relationship, it gave me confidence to listen to my deep inner knowing, opened me up to the possibility of future relationships and more importantly, demonstrated that I'm able to do what's necessary to care for myself. The memory of who I was when I made that choice remains embedded within me and resonates into future choices when I need that strength.

Intentional Choice #4 — Starting My First Entrepreneurial Venture

Choosing to start my first entrepreneurial venture was my next meaningful choice.

At thirty-two, I was let go from a big retail job while pregnant with my first child. My husband and I had just bought our first house in the suburbs that required a dual income. Initially, fear and panic coursed through every part of my body as I wondered how we'd manage financially, but I had a strong intuitive sense that being fired was a blessing. While it wasn't a choice I made for myself, but rather one that was made for me, I had the choice of how I'd react.

I could have returned to the high-paying corporate world which would have been easier, but I chose to follow my passion, step out of my self-created box and take a risk.

Leaping into the unknown and uncertain space of an entrepreneurial life was a monumental choice. Not only did it set in motion new professional opportunities, but the confidence and risk-taking I embodied in making that choice have served me through a variety of ups and downs in my years as an entrepreneur.

Intentional Choice #5 — Getting a Divorce

My fifth life-defining choice was to divorce after fifteen years of marriage.

Allan was the second man I chose to leave. One ending happened at twenty-seven, the other at forty-six. While an emotional lifetime apart, the core of my strength was similar. I was resolved and decisive, and included no one in my decision-making process.

Six months before asking for a separation, I attended an event where the speaker said, "I bet a big percentage of you are being held back in your business and life because you're in a relationship that doesn't serve you." As he uttered those prophetic words, nausea set in. I went home knowing I couldn't stay. I was not happy, we were not growing and even with therapy we couldn't find our way back to each other.

Two months after I requested the separation, Allan and I gathered our kids together in the living room we never used to break the news of our divorce. On the couch, indented from long afternoons of our dog Cosmo sleeping and watching over the house, our three children, twelve, eleven and eight, sat side by side, staring at us as we spoke.

Allan cried. I did not.

I scanned my children's faces, observing their different reactions. Beck, my middle son, smirked and tried to hide his awkward smile. Dane, my youngest, didn't really process what we shared. Tasha, my oldest, cried. She got it.

I knew Tasha wondered why I wasn't crying, and when we spoke later she asked about my lack of tears.

Wasn't I sad? Was it an easy choice for me? Did I care?

I explained that I'd made a hard choice. I was unhappy and was choosing this to take care of myself. I trusted that by feeling better I would be a better parent. I told her it was okay if she was angry with me for leaving.

"But I don't want to be angry with you," she shared.

"I know that, but it's okay if you are," I said, "You have that right. I made a choice to divorce and broke up our family as you know it."

I never wanted to presumptuously say that my choice was best for her. No one wants to be a child of divorce.

Like the choice to cancel my wedding, I straddled two worlds: one in which I knew I was taking a stand for myself, making a choice that only I could make, and the other knowing I was affecting other people's lives. I questioned: Did I know enough? Did I have enough sensitivity? Was I careless in making a choice I believed served me, but would cause hurt and pain to others?

My truth is I divorced from a place of resilience and self-care. While leaving was harrowing because it affected my family, I trusted that in choosing what I needed to support myself, my children would benefit. Like my other choices, this one created freedom and potential for what might come.

When I first got separated, one mom friend asked: Was I scared to be alone? Was I nervous about how I'd handle things financially? Was I worried about the effects of our divorce on my children? Yes, yes and yes, I answered—but not scared, nervous or worried enough to stay.

I came to realize that my divorce was a spiritual journey. Leaving was not solely about letting him go and removing the burden of a marriage that weighed me down. It's been about who I'm becoming, what I'm letting go of, how I'm taking a stand for myself, how I'm showing up for my children and sharing my truth with them, and how to have faith in what the future will bring.

Today I express that I showed up in many of my choices as "taking a stand for myself," but these are certainly not the descriptive words I'd have used in my younger days. Upon reflection, I observe that the key qualities I love about myself today were taking shape in the younger version of myself—my inner strength which allowed me to make choices without guidance or consultation, my fierce sense of independence, my keen focus on self-care and my ability to make gut-based decisions which stemmed from a deep trust and confidence in my inner knowing.

Did I have these foundational qualities in my youth? Likely not as I do in my fifties, but I can appreciate that these seeds were germinating in my younger self as evidenced by my actions. Looking back, I often wonder how I deeply understood what was best for me at such a young age? This question causes me to have greater sensitivity as a parent to ensure I honor my kids as they begin to make their own meaningful choices and trust their instincts.

When you make choices on your own, it's natural to question if you've been thoughtful and considerate as to how your actions affect others. Examining key choices with some distance can allow you to see beyond what is not well-received.

Certain choices will affect those in your life more than others, and you may waver as you realize your imminent choice has the potential to leave someone you care about reeling. This unease is an awful feeling, but it doesn't mean your choice should not be made.

By having the courage to look back, excavate your dark corners and stop telling stories that keep you mired in the past, you demonstrate your willingness to discover something about who you are that may have been previously hidden.

When you look deeply into the wisdom and lessons of your intentional choices you can discover a core part of yourself illuminated, a buried strength showing up in seemingly disparate moments. As you look at what you've chosen, you get a stronger sense of who you are. And then, as you make future choices, you can draw on the core qualities that have served you well before.

Once you've pinpointed your five intentional choices, you can plunge into a deeper investigation of each choice using the following questions. Exploring the answers to these questions will transport you back in time, providing you with a heightened awareness of who you were when you made each choice.

- What were you feeling at the time you made each choice?
- What challenges do you recall navigating as you made your decision?
- How did you feel as you considered the pros and cons of this choice?
- Did you involve others in your decision-making process?
- What positive qualities did you demonstrate in making your choice that you can now embrace and claim?
- Did you create a story about yourself because of your choice? If so, what was it?

CHAPTER 4

Your Choices Tell You Who You Are

When I was in my early twenties, I had limited experience making choices. While working for a fashion start-up, my boss, Jeff, asked me to make a decision about an assortment of garments that arrived at our overseas factory. The dresses, meant to be one color, were mistakenly a kaleidoscopic collection of cotton sheaths in a myriad of shades. Jeff asked how I wanted to handle the problem. Did I want to cancel the order, or accept the shipment and label the dresses with alternate color names?

"I don't know, I don't have enough experience to make that decision."

"You're right, you don't. Today you're twenty-four and must make your decision as a twenty-four-year-old with everything you know today. Then tomorrow, you'll use the information you gather from today's choice, plus all your other past choices, to guide you in making tomorrow's choice."

The impact Jeff's message, camouflaged in deceptively simple words, would have on my life was not one I appreciated until many years later. He gave me one of the most important gifts I've ever received—the confidence to make decisions quickly.

Each day you have many choices to make, and when you get blocked making any one of them, you hinder your ability to progress forward.

On that day many years ago, sitting in a showroom surrounded by a variety of differently-colored garments hanging on each wall, I was asked to make a choice.

And I did.

Was it the perfect choice?

Is there ever a perfect choice?

It was the best choice I could make at that moment. There were more choices to make that day, as well as in the coming days and following weeks. I kept moving through my hesitation, and with each choice felt myself growing more adept.

The beauty and gift of making each choice, no matter how small, is that it expands your arsenal of accumulated wisdom to inform your future decision-making.

Every day, you make different types of choices, from the mundane to the momentous. These choices can be categorized as simple, momentary or proactive.

Your simplest choices are those of daily living—what to eat and what to wear, for example.

If you were to stand in front of your open refrigerator questioning what to have for breakfast, getting hung up on this small daily choice, you'd create a bottleneck for the bigger ones that follow. At some point you must decide between yogurt, eggs or a smoothie. Make a choice and move on.

Your momentary choices are those that are typically binary in nature and call for more engagement than a simple choice.

Will you cook with your child or answer emails? Will you cuddle on the couch with your partner or finish cleaning the kitchen? Will you return a phone call from a friend or address the work project that needs to be completed?

Making simple and momentary choices effectively and efficiently is a muscle-building experience—the more you practice, the more confident you become in flexing this muscle to eliminate stagnation and continue moving forward. There's little risk involved in making these choices. If one causes you to go astray, it's generally straightforward to make an adjustment and course-correct.

These smaller choices don't ordinarily require much deliberation. It's when you agonize over them, getting caught in unnecessary angst and drama, that "decision fatigue" sets in and creates blockages obstructing your momentum. The most helpful question to ask when making an everyday decision is: What choice is best now? Then, visualize walking the path of each option, notice how you feel and allow your gut to be your driver.

Your proactive choices are an intentional and conscious commitment to do something that matters to you and will be the focus of this book.

With each proactive choice you either move deliberately away from something you don't want, or move toward something you're drawn to achieving or having.

Proactive choices are those you make knowing what's right for you, those that have the potential to make a great impact, those you trust will create momentum. They have greater consequences than simple and momentary choices and call for a greater level of inquiry and contemplation. Making any proactive choice, big or small, is an opportunity to affirm your values and the trajectory your life is on.

Will you choose to:

- Embrace a new opportunity?
- Open yourself to a new relationship?
- Proceed with a project that matters to you?
- Seek out a coach or therapist?
- Reach out to that person you've missed having in your life?
- Take charge of that financial issue that keeps you up at night?
- Do work that brings you joy, not just money?

Through your choices you become the person you want to be.

Should parts of your life be incompatible with what matters to you, you have two options: accept them or change them. Choosing with intention empowers you to identify what you value and take action accordingly. Making a new choice enables you to shift what is out of sync to something more aligned. With each new choice, you get to take a stand for yourself and decide how you'll respond to what comes your way. Taking stock of your choices at each turn is an indicator of whether you're moving in the right direction.

The choice is yours. The choice is always yours.

PART 2

Mapping Your Journey
How to Map

Between life and death there is a library, and within that library, the shelves go on forever. Every book provides a chance to try another life you could have lived. To see how things would be if you had made other choices… Would you have done anything different, if you had the chance to undo your regrets?

—Matt Haig, *The Midnight Library*

CHAPTER 5

Three Types of Maps

To begin your mapping journey, I want to share three Choice Mapping™ methods.

- A **People Map** documents how you know who you know.
- An **Unfolding Map** examines how a choice unfolds in your life over time.
- An **Exploration Map** provides a deeper inquiry into your emotions and the whats and whys behind your choice.

You can use these maps to examine past, present and future choices.

To create your map you can use different media, whether that's doodling in your favorite journal, typing bullet points on a Word document, creating branches in a mind-mapping software, capturing succinct words on index cards or affixing sticky notes to your kitchen wall. Regardless of the form it takes, what's unique about mapping is that it allows you to present each choice visually so you can view it from a new perspective.

As we continue through the book, I'll guide you through the inquiry and mapping process for an assortment of choices, noting specific questions that are helpful for going deeper into choices you made in the past, those you're currently making and those you're contemplating. I'll provide details of how I've used each type of map—People, Unfolding and Exploration—and will provide examples so you can delve into this process for yourself. These examples will demonstrate how this level of questioning can be applied to your life, and what it can reveal.

IMPORTANT NOTE: *There is no correct way to map, only a desire to do so.*

Much like a recipe, enjoy using the concept of the maps creatively and let them become your own. Allow the questions and guidelines to act as a springboard, a place to begin your journey, bringing fresh eyes to stories you've been telling your entire life.

In this chapter, I'll introduce you to a high-level view of the three types of maps so you can visually appreciate the different layouts. Then, in the following chapter, I'll provide examples of each type of map in action.

A People Map

A People Map is a vehicle to bring heightened awareness to how you know who you know while reflecting with gratitude on the people who facilitated those relationships.

The visual layout of this map supports you to fully appreciate the impact of one person who has introduced you to others and how those connections grow exponentially.

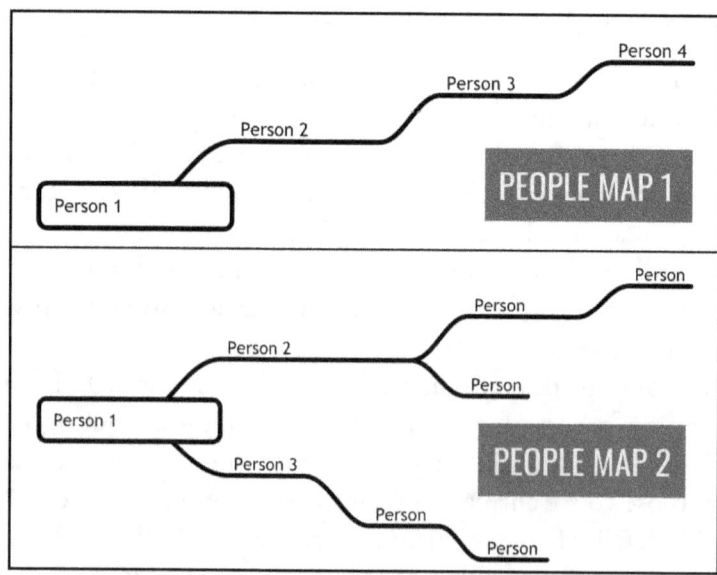

Shown on page 30 are two simple examples of People Maps. The first documents the flow from one person who connected you to another, who connected you to another and so on; the second, which is more extensive, chronicles how one person connected you to two people who then made additional connections. This map has the potential to become a living, breathing tree growing with those that are continually welcomed into your life from initial connections.

A People Map works best to review those who've connected you to others in the past and in present-time. When creating a **present-day People Map**, the source of your map will be a person who's currently connecting you to others. As you place that connector on the left of your map, you'll add branches to the right denoting evolving introductions and relationships they facilitated. From there you can further trace connections that arise from each of these branches.

To create a **past People Map**, you'll begin with one person who previously connected you to others. Branches record those you met via the original connection and will expand into present time as you continue capturing connections that emanate from the first person.

An Unfolding Map

Unfolding occurs serendipitously because of choices and changes you've decided to make; it's not something you force. With incessant distractions in your daily life, it's easy to overlook that whenever you act, your intentional, carefully chosen steps forward are mirrored by a parallel unfolding that exists outside your expectations and is beyond your control.

An Unfolding Map captures this fertile process, and is a chronological examination of all the people, opportunities, thoughts and experiences that have come into your life within a fixed period of time because of a choice you made, or are making. Structured sequentially, this map begins with your initial choice plotted on the left. Branches then expand to fill the page to the right as you capture answers to your questions of what came next, who you met and what showed up.

An Unfolding Map will help you understand how you got from one place to the next, both through your intentional actions as well as through coincidental opportunities that presented themselves. As you flesh out the branches of your map, this reflection allows you to appreciate with great gratitude and awe all that flowed into your life from one choice in a particular window of time. What happened because you chose to move, chose to begin dating a new person, chose to take the new job or because you chose to say yes to a new opportunity?

The map below depicts a simple Unfolding Map with your choice noted on the left and an expansion of thoughts, opportunities, experiences and people flowing into your life from that choice.

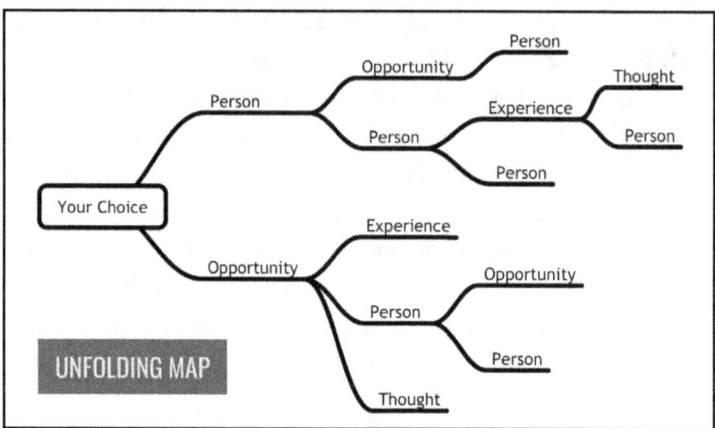

As you trace the route of each answer, you'll observe the expansive quality of one decision producing many momentum-building options. You'll notice opportunities, conversations and experiences that are obviously connected to your choice, as well as circumstances that feel tangentially aligned. Capturing these details supports you to bridge components of your life that seem unrelated, making interesting connections that, without this process, might go unnoticed.

An Unfolding Map provides a lens to focus your view of the flow that happens beyond the specific actions you've taken, illustrating how choices unfold when you allow for their momentum. Focusing on the details of an Unfolding Map elevates your awareness to all that's showing up. Noticing what's unfolding invites you to sit in a place of openness, observing and being receptive to all that materializes, relishing the uncertainty of what may come next.

With an Unfolding Map you can explore both past and present choices, and depending on the window of time you're reviewing, this type of map can be small in scope or quite boundless.

A **present-day Unfolding Map** is a useful vehicle to stay alert to the progression and synchronicities occurring because of one choice you're making now. To create your map, you'll document the choice you're currently making on the left and chronicle what's subsequently showing up with branches that expand to the right.

A **past Unfolding Map** supports you to recollect the value of all that came into your life because of a choice made months or years ago. Your map will be formed by noting a choice you made on the left and recording all the people, opportunities and experiences that showed up as a result in the branches to the right.

In Chapter Six, I'll share more detailed versions of Unfolding Maps.

An Exploration Map

The Exploration Map is guided by inquiry, rather than the chronology of an Unfolding Map. The choices best mapped with an Exploration Map are those based on an emotional goal, those that exemplify a way you want to show up, or that reflect an action you took or want to take. Will you stay on your current path or veer off to explore something new? Is the road you're traveling taking you where you want to go? Are you ready to pivot, expand and grow?

Working with an Exploration Map allows you to take the complexities of a choice and distill them into something simpler. As you pull apart an experience to unearth details and thoughts that may have been forgotten or gone unnoticed and then reassemble the pieces, you open yourself to discerning new levels of wisdom.

The Exploration Map is the one I gravitate to most often and is in large part the main focus for the balance of the book. The information garnered in this type of map enables you to stand in the strength of all you've learned, all you've experienced, all you've become and all you know. It is an invaluable instrument to explore all choices.

In a **past Exploration Map**, you'll delve into a previous choice to look at who you were, seeking to understand what motivated you and what you learned as a result. This map will provide you with a vehicle for in-depth inquiry, inviting your curious mind into what's not been explored before. Exploration Maps can be used to retell stories from the past with a wiser perspective that allows you to release pain and find new meaning.

A **present-day Exploration Map** and a **future Exploration Map** will provide you with a means to dive into an interactive dialogue about why you're making (or want to make) a specific choice, what you're scared of, how you want to show up, what's possible and what actions you'll take.

The most valuable aspect of the Exploration Map is that it provides a framework to think through a choice that's clear and succinct yet rich with insight. As you examine why you're making a particular choice, you'll candidly assess what fears or limiting beliefs may be getting in your way of fully stepping into that choice.

At its simplest, an Exploration Map begins with seeking answers to five core questions which have a subtly different flavor depending on if you're looking back to a past choice, or are contemplating a present or future choice.

To dissect a past choice, you'll reflect on the following questions:

1. Why did you make this choice?

2. What fears did you have to overcome to step into this choice?

3. How did you feel when you made this choice?

4. What did you hope would happen?

5. What did you learn about yourself from this choice?

To bring deeper focus and examination to a present or future choice you're considering, you'll reflect on these questions:

1. Why does this choice matter to you?

2. What fears (or limiting beliefs) might get in your way of stepping into the choice?

3. How do you want to show up as you make your decision?

4. What may become possible because you make this choice?

5. What actions will you take to bring your choice to life?

During this process of curious investigation, your inquiry will stem from a desire to stay cognizant of everything you're doing related to a specific present-day choice. Mapping choices as you live them fosters staying conscious of your thoughts and actions as well as what could block you so you can address these impediments objectively.

Immersing yourself in the creation of a **present-day Exploration Map** empowers you to engage in a dialogue with yourself, synthesizing the answers you capture into digestible nuggets that reveal new insights, while keeping the elements of your choice in the forefront of your thoughts. Placing focused energy in the details of your choice imbues them with meaning. As you engage in the inquiry process, you infuse your actions with a thoughtfulness that demonstrates your personal buy-in.

Each map invites you to savor the question-and-answer process, and supports you to stay truthful and centered about your motivation for why you do what you do.

With a greater clarity about why your choice matters, you're laying the foundation to put your full resources toward your actions. Your aspiration is to stay conscious, alert and committed to the actions you take that continue to support your choice to move forward. Using your map as a guide allows you to envision your actions and responses to what comes up along the way.

As I guide you through the mapping experience, I'll provide direction and thoughts about how to best contemplate each of these five questions. (See the table on page 37 noting how to best find that content.) I'll furnish you with examples of others' answers and make suggestions for ways to take your personal exploration deeper. And, I'll provide examples from the simple to the more complex.

While an Exploration Map visually begins with your choice as its hub, sprouting outward-reaching branches, there are options as to how you orient your Exploration Map.

One is to orient your map like a tree where the roots are formed by the first two questions regarding why the choice matters and which fears may affect your choice. The next three questions about how you'll show up, what's possible for you and the actions you'll take face upward, forming your branches. (*See Exploration Map 1 on the next page.*)

Another option, which is the one I typically use, is to orient your map horizontally, with your questions beginning at the top left and moving to the top right. (*See Exploration Map 2 on the next page.*)

Although the five core questions of a past choice differ slightly, the visual framework of the Exploration Map remains the same. The past choice you're investigating will sit in the map's center. The branches, which extend like spokes, will document the answers to how, what and why questions.

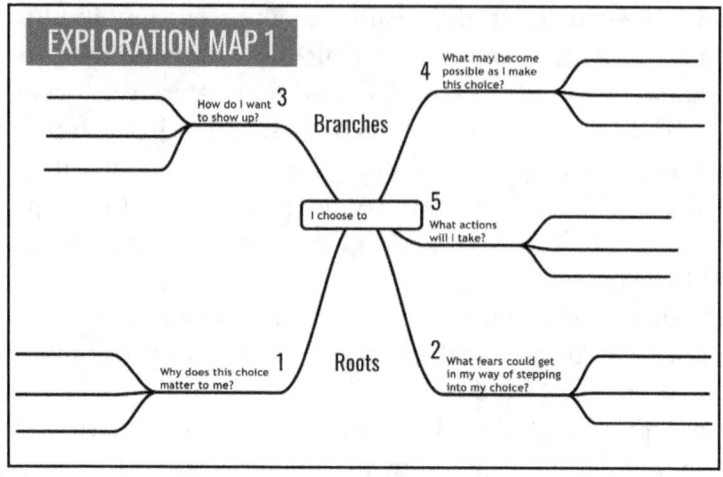

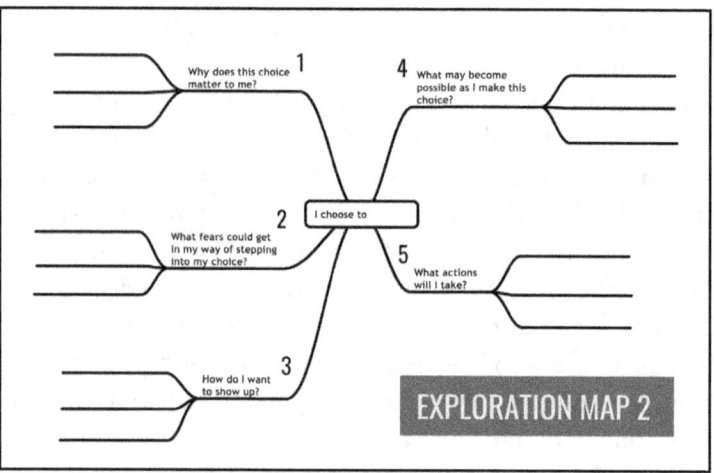

Remember, there is no correct way to map, only a desire to do so. Avail yourself of this tool I'm sharing and make it your own, discovering what makes sense and provides you with the most value.

To watch instructional videos on the map-making process, visit http://kimdeyoung.com/ChoiceResources.

On the next page you'll find the Exploration Map questions organized into a table. For now, as you're just getting acquainted with mapping, the most important thing to grasp is the questions themselves. Later in the book, I devote a chapter to each Exploration

Map question, expanding it and showing you how to work with it in greater detail. If you want to dig into one question, the table on the following page will guide you to the right place.

Where to Find More Information on Each Exploration Map Question	Chapter
Why does this choice matter to you?	8
What fears could get in your way of stepping into your choice?	9
How do you want to show up as you make your choice?	10
What may become possible because you make this choice?	21
What limiting beliefs could hold you back?	21
What actions will you take to bring your choice to life?	22

CHAPTER 6

Maps in Action

Since creating this Choice Mapping™ process, I've used it as a powerful tool to disentangle the details of my choices and help my friends, family and clients unravel theirs. Looking at your choices impartially allows you to take responsibility for your actions. This technique supports you to hold yourself accountable for your thoughts as well as the consequences of your various decisions. Examining these with an eye to clarity and integrity allows you to continually learn from and apply the lessons of your choices.

In this chapter, I share examples from my actual maps as well as those of friends and clients. As you view these maps and how they were created, consider how you can apply the shared concepts to your choices.

People Maps in Action

I've always enjoyed noting how I know who I know. As new people enter my life, I often ask myself, *how was I lucky enough to meet them? Who led me to them?*

A few years ago, I began having chronic pain in my hip and the owner of my gym, Christa, referred me to Francine, her chiropractor. After continuing to feel lots of discomfort, Francine forwarded me on to an orthopedist who requested I get x-rays. As the x-ray tech and I chatted about our health, she glowingly spoke of the healing she'd received from her naturopath Elise. I called Elise immediately.

What began as a patient/client relationship grew into me offering to explore a choice Elise wanted to make. Her interest in what I did prompted me to share my initial chapters of this book. Her comments and direction were so intuitive, sensitive and insightful that I asked her to contribute her energy and wisdom as my book coach and editor. Not only is Elise's beautiful presence felt within the pages of this book, she's also been an integral part of my hip's healing journey.

This People Map simply denotes the flow from Christa to Elise, one step leading seamlessly to the next. Creating the map brought each person to mind, allowing me to reconnect with my gratitude for their connections. This map allowed me to emotionally bridge Christa and Elise, two special women in my life, who while they don't know each other, were each instrumental in guiding me along my path.

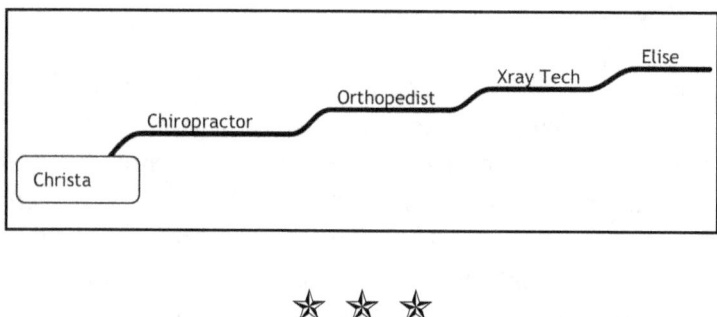

✳ ✳ ✳

The idea for this book and the beginning of my mapping journey began after an important romantic relationship came to an end. As part of my uncoupling process, I wanted to feel gratitude for what we had and what he'd opened up in me so I could let him go and ultimately move on.

I had a sense that Mark had connected me to many people during and after our relationship, but I couldn't quantify the number. Wanting to visualize his positive impact, I created my first People Map documenting the many people who came into my life because of his initial introductions.

In the course of our relationship, Mark introduced me to fourteen people for both professional and personal reasons. From those fourteen connections I met another sixty people who became business partners and friends.

Mark occupies the root on the left side of the map with fourteen branches expanding from him, each representing a connection he made between me and another. In the map pictured here, each line is filled with a person's name. Details are blurred intentionally, as the focus right now is the big picture of the People Map.

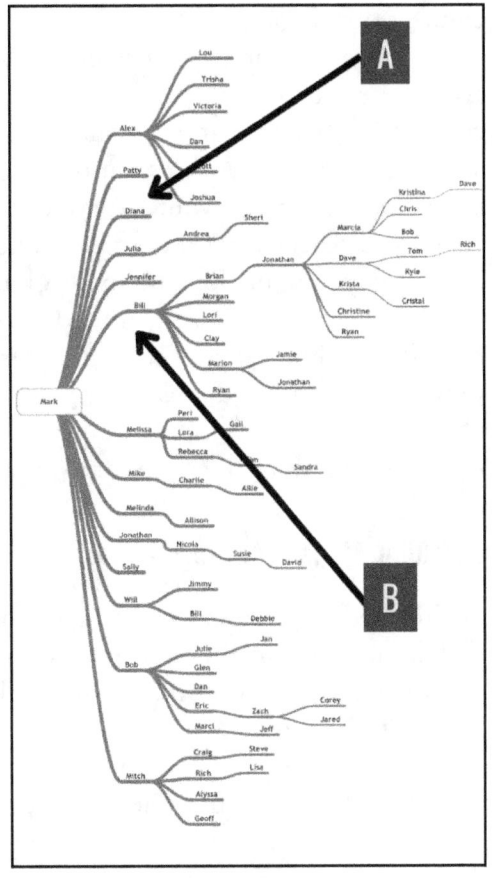

Some of the connections were a sweet introduction which went no further, so no additional branches emanated (see Arrow A). Others took on a life of their own, and from one connection more branches with new people extended outward (see Arrow B).

I created this map to provide myself with a visual tool to gratefully acknowledge all the people that entered my life because of Mark. I knew it was significant, but once the map was complete I was astounded to see, visually represented on one piece of paper, the breadth of his impact in many different areas of my life. The people represented in this map have become the core of my social and professional world.

Viewing a People Map in this way allows you to fully appreciate the power and impact of one person. Creating a People Map demonstrates how a choice to embark on a relationship with one person has the potential to create great momentum, both in your life and in the lives of others. Each interaction causes a chain reaction of occurrences—someone you barely knew can become a conduit to a lineage of new connections.

My choice to embark on a relationship with Mark created a huge ripple that stretches into the present where I continually add new people to my map—people who spring from the seed of our initial connection.

The People Map illustrates not only the impact of one person, but also where momentum is stunted. Are there opportunities for greater connection that have gone dormant? (See Arrow A in the map on page 41.) Are there relationships you'd like to renew, or plans you'd like to make that strengthen your network of connectedness? A People Map allows you to determine whether connections have ended with intention, or gone unpursued due to life's busyness.

You'll see this concept again in Unfolding Maps, which capture not just people, but experiences, thoughts and opportunities that have shown up over time. Maps allow you to see, visually, where things left off, and you have the opportunity to bring attention back to them whenever you want to create some movement.

Unfolding Maps in Action

To guide your understanding of the basic structure of maps, the Unfolding Maps in this section have been simplified. For now, you'll want to get a sense of the map framework without getting bogged down in details.

My first map, which explored my choice to attend the coaching workshop that I shared in the introduction, was an Unfolding Map. In this map, beginning on the left and moving out to the right, I captured the chronology of people, experiences and opportunities that presented themselves in a two-year window.

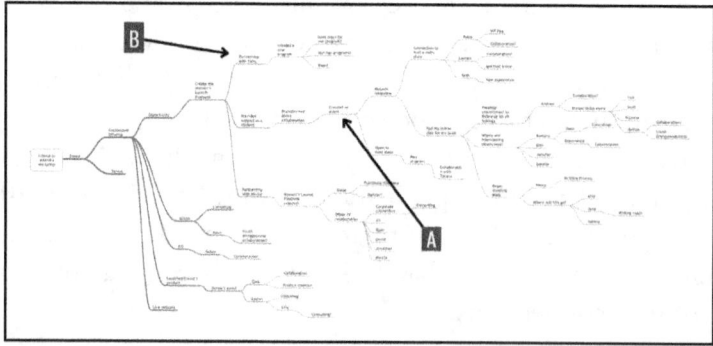

In the aerial view of this map, you can see the breadth of activity and expansion that's possible from one choice. As I continually asked myself *"what showed up next?"* I recalled information that allowed branches to spread across the page. For some of what came into my life, I took action to make it happen—actively connecting with someone or following up on an opportunity. In other instances, opportunities, people and ideas presented themselves without force and effort.

Arrow A on page 42 shows the mushrooming of people and opportunities that occurred after I had the initial vision for this book. Upon the book's conception, I made the commitment to pursue all inklings, no matter how small or strange. A soft whisper nudged me to contact a man I barely knew. Our conversation led him to invite me to attend his business event, which led to new connections and opportunities. Documenting these connections in an Unfolding Map allowed me to pause and reflect on each person and relish our experience together.

While an Unfolding Map is an invaluable tool to deeply appreciate all that has occurred within a fixed window in the past, it's also a vehicle to generate movement in the present if you're feeling stuck. *Arrow B* on page 42 denotes a branch that's abruptly halted. At that time, I was in conversation with a colleague about next steps for a project but I was remiss about follow-up so our plans stalled. The halt represents inaction and lack of attention. This is similar to what we saw with People Maps in the prior section. These maps can show opportunities for growth by making clear where expansion is and is not happening. If I wanted to instigate momentum and continue the expansion of branches, I could initiate a call to this colleague to generate forward motion.

In her twenties, my good friend, Anna, wrestled with big existential questions—how life works, why relationships go awry and what her life's purpose was. As a spiritually hungry young woman, she made a financial and emotional leap to attend a weekend event, eager for conversation and hoping for answers to some of her big questions.

Twenty years later, interested to reflect on what had come into her life from this transformative experience, I created Anna's Unfolding Map (seen on the following page) to capture the growth and challenges she sustained.

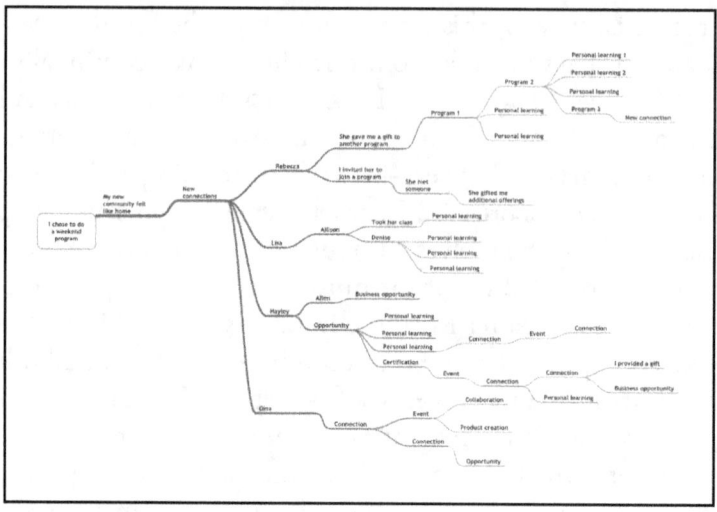

Her new relationships with people she met at the weekend event became the community she never had within her fractured family of origin. These friendships led to personal and business opportunities which created branches upon branches. Observing her life through the lens of this event, Anna witnessed that many of her life's opportunities and much of her personal growth stemmed from people met and connections made decades earlier. She could trace her resolve to take greater responsibility for her actions, no longer show up as a victim and not take things personally, directly back to connections made at the event.

An Unfolding Map is a useful tool to document all that's showing up in real time from a choice you've recently made, supporting you to stay present to what's flowing in.

Years ago, I hired a spiritual coach, sensing much would come from our work together. I created my first "live" Unfolding Map to document all that transpired throughout my time with her. After each weekly session, I spent a few contemplative moments adding branches of amassed thoughts, resources and experiences. From those resources, I followed the threads to people, books, websites and synchronicities. This image captures a two-month window of breadcrumbs I followed that might have gone unnoticed had I not captured them in a map.

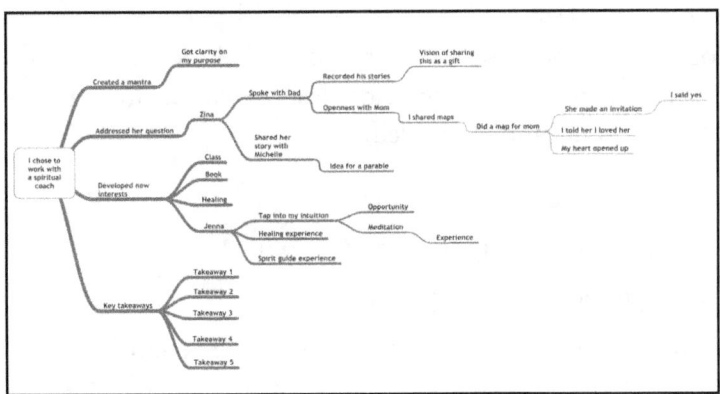

I've since incorporated this concept into a treasured ritual. Every morning before the craze of my day begins, I devote a few quiet moments to nurturing a live Unfolding Map. During this time, I spend typically no more than five minutes reflecting on the people, opportunities, synchronicities and experiences I've either intentionally brought into my life or that have coincidentally shown up because of a choice I've recently made. Should you find meditation difficult, this practice is an accessible alternative to finding space for quiet contemplation and learning how to be an observer.

This simple practice has the potential to heighten your level of gratitude and sharpen your awareness to the details and subtleties you're manifesting, that without this practice, might fall below your radar and therefore not be appreciated. With an Unfolding Map, you can visually appreciate how much is before you at a given point in time.

Exploration Maps in Action

As you seek to go deeper with your inquiry, an Exploration Map provides you with a vehicle to ask and then answer questions in a call-and-response manner, peeling back layers of story to uncover your truth.

An Exploration Map provides a format for re-telling a story. Unraveling the salient pieces of your stories and reassembling them from different vantage points can reinvigorate each story with new life and meaning. Your words and unearthed gems become the building blocks for new narration—an opportunity to reframe what may have been a story you were uncomfortable with, ashamed of or had simply forgotten.

To open your thoughts to the breadth of choices to explore, here are examples of personal, professional and relationship choices I've explored with others and for myself:

- Choosing to start an entrepreneurial venture
- Choosing to embark upon a creative journey
- Choosing to begin a yoga practice
- Choosing to say yes to something that interests you
- Choosing to heal and learn from a past relationship
- Choosing to have a baby
- Choosing to begin dating
- Choosing to work with a coach or therapist
- Choosing to write a book
- Choosing to shift gears professionally
- Choosing to do reconstructive surgery
- Choosing to attend a workshop
- Choosing to sell a home
- Choosing to leave a marriage
- Choosing to join a coaching group
- Choosing to move away from family and friends
- Choosing to retire
- Choosing to stop telling unhealthy stories

At every age and stage, you have an opportunity to navigate those choices presented to you, those that happen to you and those you intentionally create. Making proactive choices with consciousness is an opportunity to affirm your values.

In this section, I present a handful of Exploration Maps and questions to provide a guide as you begin. Where appropriate, I share my recollection of the dialogue I had with my clients to provide context so you can imagine yourself answering similar questions.

The first example models a simple, and I believe, relatable choice many of us face so I can share the basics of how to use this more involved map type. Imagine making the choice to add a healthy habit to your life. The first branch of your Exploration Map will focus on why that choice matters to you.

Perhaps your answers or reasons are something like this:

- I want to feel healthier.

- I want to take my well-being seriously.

The second branch will explore any fears or limiting beliefs that could get in the way of making your choice a reality. As this is a fairly widespread choice, I've often heard answers like:

- I fear I will slack off on my commitment and feel bad about myself.

- I fear that I don't have the wherewithal to make a change.

- I've tried to do this kind of thing before and failed. Why will it be any different this time?

The third branch will explore how you'll choose to show up as you make this decision.

- I'll show up committed.

- I'll show up confident that I can make this change.

The fourth branch will explore what's possible for you because of this choice.

- I'll feel better about myself.

- I'll know that I'm capable.

And the final branch will explore the actions you plan to take regarding this choice.

- I'll prepare my environment the night before so I'm set up to succeed.

- I'll link my new habit to a habit I already do each day so it's easier to remember.

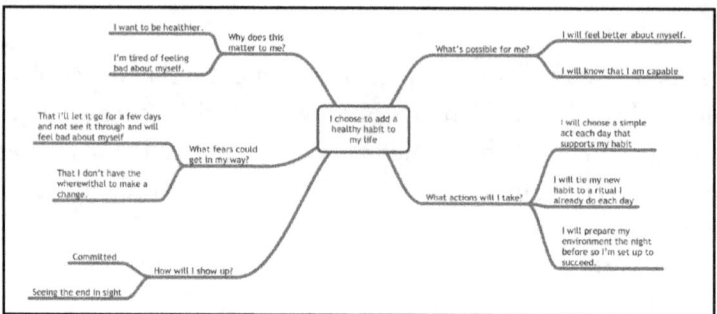

To get comfortable using an Exploration Map, take a few moments and explore this particular example for yourself, noting your answers to these questions. What does choosing to create a healthy habit look like for you? As you seek to answer the five key questions, what words will you place on your map's branches?

The following Exploration Maps exemplify the questions I asked two clients who chose to move away from a life they knew to one that called to them. One wanted to revel in the personal strength she exhibited at a youthful age, the other was contemplating a bold move to reinvent herself in mid-life.

Marla, a strong, independent woman in her thirties with a career that mattered to her, wanted to examine a choice made a decade earlier. In her twenties, she felt a compelling intuitive nudge to leave her stable teaching job on the East Coast and move abroad.

"Why did this choice matter to you?" I inquired.

"While I had everything in my then current life—a stable job, good pay and supportive friendships, I wanted more. I knew there was something for me overseas and while I didn't know what it was, I was open to new opportunities for what I'd do and where I'd live."

"What fears do you recall having?" I probed.

"Many in my family felt betrayed, which caused me to question if I was doing the right thing. As much as I felt guilty about leaving, I feared if I didn't make a move, I'd stay the same for the next thirty years. I feared if I stayed, the path laid out before me would be to ultimately buy a home and have two kids. This was not what I wanted. While I knew leaving would cause me to be alienated from my family, I still chose to do it."

"Did anyone support your choice?" I asked.

"My mother told me to follow my dreams, that I'd only have them once. I remember my boss asking if I was sure I was doing the right thing. I told him I was and he kindly agreed to hold my job for the year so I had no risk in leaving. With no tethers holding me back, the timing was perfect and with each step I took, the bridge behind me fell away until I had no net."

Marla acknowledged and recognized her fears but felt the call of the unknown was more intriguing than the fear of what she was leaving behind. The possibility of what awaited beckoned her into the future.

The map below shows the aerial view of Marla's Exploration Map. The details of her specific map have been replaced with words that describe the type of content on each branch—people, opportunity, fear, etc.—to keep the focus on the map skeleton, which is what is important here.

The expansiveness of the upper right branch validates the excitement Marla felt regarding what could become possible as she stepped into this choice, as indicated by the arrow below.

✸ ✸ ✸

After living in the same area for much of her life, my client Jenna, a fifty-year old empty-nester, was ready for a change and craved a new foundation upon which to build her life.

Knowing she had the flexibility to work wherever she had a phone and computer, Jenna was in search of adventure and excitement in both her personal and professional lives. At the center of her Exploration Map she stated: *I choose to explore moving to a new city.*

Using the word *explore* in her declaration softened Jenna's choice, providing a buffer. It felt safer to begin her map with that statement rather than the decisiveness of: *I choose to move to a new city.*

"Why does this choice matter to you?" I asked.

"My old world has grown unpleasantly familiar," she explained. "I feel stagnant and sense that if I don't make an imminent change I'll become withdrawn and insular."

"What scares you as you consider this move?" I inquired.

Jenna candidly shared her fears about the unknown—who she'd meet, how she'd build a community and her concern of being alone. Although she was apprehensive about having so much uncertainty in her life, continuing in the status quo was more painful.

We continued to explore a series of inquiries to delve into her choice: why she wanted to move, the anxiety she felt around the uncertainty of leaving, her apprehension about what might happen if she didn't make this change and the many specifics of what she dreamt of in a new location.

Her map (seen on the following page) held equal parts fear around what was unknown and excitement about what was possible. The fears of whether she would be lonely and how she would create community filled one set of branches. The excitement of new romance, new friends and new activities filled another.

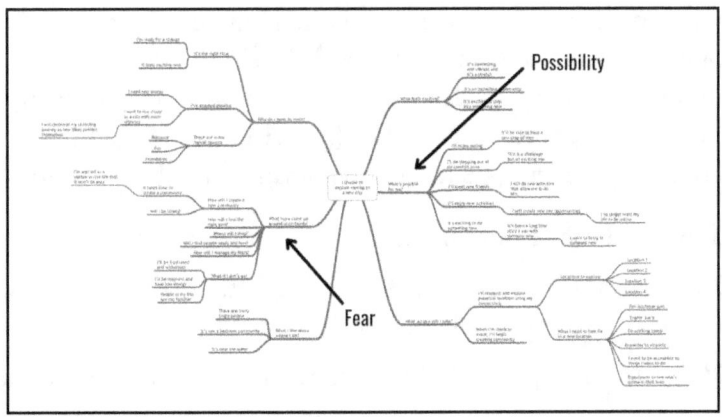

Clarifying the specifics she wanted in a new location, from a women-owned gym, to a nearby Trader Joe's, to a coworking space, allowed Jenna to research and explore potential locations using her network. After posing the question of where to move to her friends on social media, she received a multitude of intriguing suggestions and began exploring unexpected cities. She embarked on a journey to follow the breadcrumbs, which created a dynamic pull into newness that felt exciting and magnetic.

As Jenna navigated the breadth of emotions related to leaving, the map provided a useful tool to ground her in the hurdles she needed to overcome as well as the lure of what felt exciting. Although she felt frightened to let go of what was secure and familiar, she began to imagine what was possible for her life in a way that extended beyond a literal move. By turning her gaze to all the possibilities with a sense of openness, she, like Marla, created momentum around her desire for change and transformation, and invited it to present itself in unexpected ways.

After doing many Exploration Maps for others, I turned my gaze inward to use this tool to understand who I was as a twenty-year-old when I chose to expand my major to include Art History. In creating my *Art History as a Turning Point* Exploration Map, I sought to gain greater visibility into my motivation, fears, limiting beliefs and dreams.

Using an approach of deep and sustained curiosity, I took the series of Exploration Map questions to a deeper level.

I began my map by reflecting upon six questions, capturing concise answers on six expanding branches (Note: I added an additional question about my limiting beliefs knowing this was a big issue for me.)

- Why did I make this choice?
- What fears did I have to break through that could have prevented me from making the choice?
- What limiting beliefs did I need to reframe so I could move forward?
- How had I shown up at that time?
- What did I think might happen?
- How did this choice affect my life?

With each question I excavated more, eagerly anticipating where the trail of my answers would lead. Faithfully, I listened, noticed and trusted I would uncover a richer sense of meaning embedded in layers of story, memory and perception.

While I initially feared taking Art History 101, imagining it consisted solely of memorizing the dates of paintings, it became apparent that the study of art is a beautiful amalgamation of sociology, psychology, religion, history and art. Incredibly drawn to its multi-layered character, making this choice was my first strong inner knowing that I must move forward, regardless of the consequences.

To explore what caused me anxiety as I stepped into this choice, one map's branch examined how I felt fearing my father's disapproval. Another branch delved into how making this choice caused me to view myself, as well as how others would see me. A third reflected upon: Was I making a huge mistake that could hurt me academically and limit my professional options?

My life to that point was governed by being a smart, "good" girl who followed directions, listened and did the right thing. By breaking the rules and expanding my major beyond Economics, the major my father suggested and approved of, had I shifted to become a "bad" girl?

With little experience in trusting my intuition, I had an innate sense of what was right for me, and I observed that I was willing to go head-to-head with my dad if he disagreed.

"Kim," my father incredulously asked, "what will you do with an Art History degree? Sit around in coffee shops speaking about Rembrandt?"

Deflecting his sarcastic comment, I shared with deep conviction that I saw myself combining business with creativity and was interested in working with an art auction house. I felt incredibly empowered knowing I'd constructed a new avenue for my education that wasn't dictated by his beliefs.

Creating this map allowed me to own that this choice was my first recollection of truly asserting my independence—stepping away from my father, showing him, and more importantly, demonstrating to myself that I could make a decision that mattered to me regardless of how he felt. Although I don't believe at twenty I sat with all this insight as consciously as I describe with a present-day adult perspective, I do recall internalizing a sense of great self-reliance and strength that remains embodied within me. The mapping process demonstrated with considerable certainty that my choice was a pivotal step in my development of independence and self-confidence.

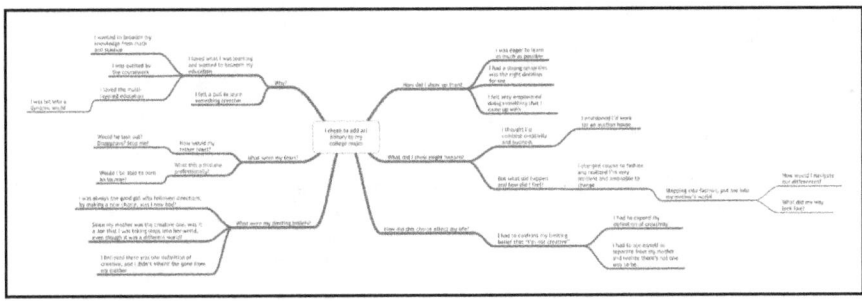

CHAPTER 7

Taking Maps Deeper

Now that we've waded into the waters of map making, I'd like to invite you to swim a little deeper—to go on a journey with me and my clients as well as some friends and family using the map you just learned about, the Exploration Map. Of the various map options, Exploration Maps will be the primary method used to take stock of your choices making it a great place to deepen your understanding of mapping.

As we move through the book, we'll examine three time-frames of choices:

- Those choices you're making today (Part 3)
- Those choices you've made in your past (Part 4)
- And those choices you're contemplating making in the future. (Part 5)

Examining a choice through an Exploration Map allows you to find your way, understanding yourself through thoughtful questioning, revealing a truth beyond what you've told yourself and presenting insights that support you to have greater empathy for who you are today. By creating Exploration Maps, you can probe details of your personal history as well as your present choices. You'll learn more about who you were and see your guiding lights more clearly.

As you enter into the experience of Exploration Mapping, the two most important questions to reflect upon are:

1. Why does this choice matter to you?

2. What fears could get in your way of stepping into this choice?

These two questions will be the root of your map and form its structure.

These next three questions then create the extending branches of your map:

3. How do you want to show up as you make your decision?

4. What may become possible because you make this choice?

5. What actions will you take to bring your choice to life?

Once you've answered the five broader questions, you can lean in with more pointed questions. The continued question-and-answer process will broaden the growth of your map.

- What does making this choice say about you?

- What's the cost of not making this choice?

- What is it worth to you to make this choice?

When I began my coaching training, I quickly learned that the quality of my coaching was contingent upon the quality of my questions. I observed that the skill of a truly adept coach is not to provide solutions but to pose powerful questions that draw out the client's wisdom, enabling them to look inward and discover that they have the answers for themselves.

As children we possess an innate curiosity and natural ability to question. We make sense of the world by asking "why" questions. As we grow, we continue asking versions of these questions—*Why* did I do that? *Why* is this happening to me? *Why* aren't I more of this or less of that?

Questions focused on *why* orient our gaze toward the past, often causing us to feel defensive and judged.

Alternatively, asking "what" questions directs our view toward the future as we gather information and seek a solution. *What* is it I want? *What* fears are preventing me from taking action? *What* matters to me?

What questions generally have a kinder underlying tone and elicit more open-hearted, action-oriented answers. They produce information that's less emotionally charged, freeing us from feeling criticized and becoming embroiled in blame and defensiveness.

Asking questions to navigate your choices is an art without a strict formula—there's no singular or correct way to do it. A good question expands your thinking and widens your perspective. It sparks an internal dialogue that draws you past the tide of emotion toward your core values. Good questions are nonjudgmental. They seek information to create a fuller emotional picture around your choice which counteracts the tendency to overemphasize the difficult or problematic aspects. Addressing key questions clearly and honestly before making an important choice provides greater ammunition for determining what's at stake.

Asking well-crafted "what" questions is essential to generating helpful answers. In the process of making a deliberate choice, thoughtful questions fuel your brain's fact-finding ability, helping to uncover your truth.

A friend who runs her own business was disappointed about not having increased her revenue as she anticipated. Her cycle of asking disdainful *why* questions dragged her through past doubts and invalidation, leaving her to feel disillusioned.

- Why didn't I host my group coaching program when I had the chance?
- Why did I get in my own way?
- Why haven't I generated more clients?

To generate more supportive answers, I suggested she reframe her wording:

- What would it take to host a new program?
- What's getting in your way of doing what you want?
- What actions could you take to move toward what matters to you?

Changing questions from *why* to *what* triggers your brain to conceive favorable and actionable answers. It reorients you to the present where you have control over what happens next, shedding the heaviness and condemnation inherent in asking *why*.

Asking yourself powerful "*what*" questions supports you to go deeper than the five core Exploration Map questions to continue drawing out your wisdom and insights.

As you become more inquisitive, learning to let go of assumptions in favor of flexing your muscles of curiosity, take time to listen carefully for your answers, treating each one as a step bringing you closer toward your truth. While you engage in an internal dialogue, trust that everything you need to guide you is within you waiting to be uncovered.

As you seek greater understanding of your motivations and desires prior to making a proactive choice, you have an opportunity to draw yourself out by asking well-crafted questions. Just as we crave deep connection to others, we crave deep awareness and connection to ourselves. Learning to ask thoughtful and probing questions rooted in honest curiosity is a habit and practice that builds upon itself, allowing you to uncover your truth and shift your perspective. Each time you embark upon an internal question-and-answer dialogue you train yourself to be your own guide.

In the following example, I asked myself *what* questions to guide my thinking and support myself to express my emotions more clearly after feeling triggered by a boyfriend's simple question.

"Is there a reason you left the spoon on the counter?" he asked.

His words, which felt like a passive-aggressive dig, sent me into a tailspin. Feeling embarrassed and childlike, I retreated. After a night of fitful sleep, I woke to process my thoughts, frustrated that I'd let the undercurrent of his question, and my inability to speak properly about how it affected me, drive a wedge between us.

Cozying up on his couch as morning light filled his den, I opened my laptop to create a new Exploration Map stating in the center: *I choose to get to the root of what triggered me.*

Branches extended with my queries:

- *What* did his words make me feel?

- *What* am I making this interaction mean?

- *What* behaviors am I exhibiting that are similar to my childhood?

My questions left no room for excuses or defensive behaviors—they requested a truthful answer. Wanting to deliberately coach myself out of a funk into a space where I could engage in a calm and productive conversation, I guided myself with neutral, curious language.

As I followed the trail of my answers, I was flooded with emotions which I let surge to the surface and into the branches of my map. I felt like a child who'd been reprimanded for being dirty and careless. I was embarrassed that he'd witnessed a messier part of me when my outward-facing self is competent, clean and put together. I felt invalidated, as if the years I'd single-handedly run a household with three children had no relevance. I was irritated that his words were not more direct: "Next time, please put your spoon in the sink." My automatic reaction was to withdraw, stewing behind a closed door—the same way I'd seen conflicts handled in my childhood. Changing that response required awareness and resolve to undo.

Allowing focused *what* questions to guide my process, this relatively simple Exploration Map supported me to gain clarity about how I was feeling so I could communicate more effectively. In the light of a new day, armed with layers of details about my emotions, I used the information I'd gathered in my personal answer-seeking experience to clearly express why I'd withdrawn, how I planned to shift and to ask that he speak more directly in the future.

So that you can continually challenge and stimulate yourself to ask coach-worthy questions, as we move deeper into the book I'll provide many examples across a breadth of choices—sharing how to delve into your present-day choices to assess what motivates you, what may trigger you and what actions you're willing to take. We'll look with compassion at your past choices to gain insights that support you in healing any shame or disappointment you've endured as a result of a perceived bad decision. We'll see through examples that acknowledging, and then owning your truth bolsters you to enter your next phase with greater confidence.

What's Ahead...

Let me orient you to the journey I'll be guiding you on for the balance of the book.

I'll provide more detailed explanations for how to utilize the five key questions to create an Exploration Map, and show you examples of how others have used them.

In Part 3, as we look at your **present choices**, I'll be focusing on the first three questions.

- We'll examine the first and most important question as you begin any Exploration Map: *Why does this choice matter to you?*

- Next we'll dive into the second question: *What fears could get in your way of stepping into your choice?*

- Then I'll introduce you to a new way to think about: *How do you want to show up as you make your choice?*

- As we wrap up this section, I'll share a bonus tool about how to use your intuition to support you in reviewing your questions.

In Part 4, we'll look back at your **past choices** and the stories you've created because of those choices. What did you hope for, how did you make your choice, what was its impact and what did you learn? We'll look at what it takes to release any shame and guilt you've held onto because of choices you've viewed as "bad."

As we move into Part 5, focusing primarily on **future choices**, we'll explore the final two Exploration Map questions:

- *What may become possible because you make this choice?*

- And, *what actions will you take to bring your choice to life?*

PART 3

Present Choices
Acting with Intention

*At any moment, the decision you make can
change the course of your life forever.*
—Tony Robbins

CHAPTER 8

Present-Day Maps in Action

We'll begin our focus in this section by looking at the proactive choices you're making now, in present-time.

Proactive choices are significant—with each one you're making an intentional commitment to do something that matters to you. You're either moving toward something you're drawn to achieving or having, or moving away from something you don't want.

With each proactive choice, your aim is to stay conscious, alert and committed to the actions you take that support your choice to move forward. Using an Exploration Map as a guide encourages you to assess what could undermine your efforts so you can plot your actions and responses accordingly.

Intentional, proactive choices typically fall into three categories:

1. **For professional choices** you're determining whether to start or leave a job, step out on your own or improve your current situation.

2. **In relationship choices** you're focusing on whether to begin a new relationship, work on mending one you're already in or end one that is no longer fulfilling.

3. **Your personal choices** involve bringing something into your life that matters or removing something that doesn't. You may choose to move, embrace a new opportunity, write a book or bring joy into your life. As you seek growth and development,

you may choose to address something that bothers you, reframe an old, unhealthy story into one that's more supportive or work with a new coach or therapist.

The specific choices you can make within each category are vast and at any given time you may be managing multiple choices across these categories. You may be choosing to start a new job while concurrently ending a personal relationship while choosing to begin a morning meditation practice. You may be choosing to work with a new therapist while choosing to begin dating while also choosing to give greater attention to your self-care.

As we move through Part 3, which covers present choices, we'll explore examples, questions and maps within these three categories (professional, relationship and personal choices).

For now, the main takeaway is that any of these choices is best mapped using an Exploration Map.

Each Exploration Map begins with the foundational question: **Why does this choice matter to you?** From this question, your mapping journey begins, allowing you to assess if your reasons are compelling enough to invest your energy in this decision.

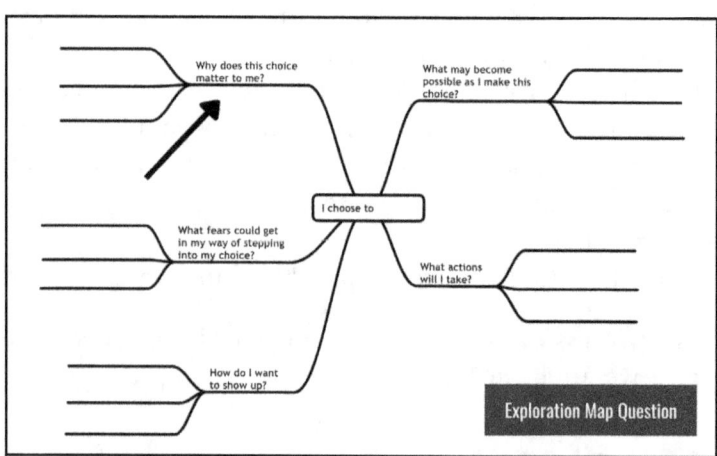

I've given you a map template above as a visual example of how to use the Exploration Map questions. As the arrow indicates, in this section, we're focusing on the first question: *Why does this choice matter to you?* Throughout the course of the book, you'll see this template again as we work with each of the additional Exploration Map questions.

For now, to get familiar working with this one leg of the Exploration Map, you'll see snippets from the other people's maps. So that you can get accustomed to utilizing the question of why this choice matters to you, here are a few examples of how clients, friends and family have answered this question across a handful of personal, professional and relationship choices:

- Liza chose to close down a holistic health practice she'd owned for years. This choice mattered to her because she'd become resentful that her current practice took time away from another venture she dreamt of starting.

- As Elaine ended a relationship, she chose to take a stand for herself, which mattered because she'd always conformed to other people's desires in order to feel lovable. She was ready to no longer defer to others in order to gain approval.

- Adam chose to lead a group coaching program, which mattered to him because he felt burnt out by the drain of private one-to-one client work, and because he wanted his business to reach a broader audience.

- Kaia was at a pivotal point in her life. She had married young and was recently divorced. She was ready to make her own choices and let go of allowing others to control her life.

As you're becoming familiar with how to start an Exploration Map for a present choice, I'll take you behind the scenes of three choices I made during the writing of this book. I first addressed why the choice mattered to me, and subsequently asked a number of questions to peel back layers to reach the deep underbelly of what could have held me back from doing what mattered.

Present Choice 1

My journey of writing this book was fraught with stops and starts. A year into the process I made the present choice to stop writing, not knowing how long that choice might last. I had a strong intuitive sense that the book, which I'd originally envisioned would share the learning garnered from exploring other people's choices, needed to be expanded to incorporate the wisdom and process I'd extracted from creating many personal maps. How might I do that when I created each of my maps with the rawness of a private journal that I never imagined sharing?

How, I wondered as I stepped into the personal experience of writing my book, would I accomplish letting you into the inner workings of my maps and expose my unfiltered, vulnerable thoughts?

Knowing I could not continue until I found my way, I chose to sit with this question and withdraw from my writing. I asked how I might share my personal process and open a door to reveal what would be supportive to you, while not baring all. How would I provide the value of going deep and being truthful while maintaining a sense of privacy? Which pieces of my stories and thought processes could I present and share so they'd be relevant insights for you?

Before I could examine the fear and get excited about the possibilities, I wanted to address why my choice mattered. Only then could I consider the nervousness and potential outcomes around what might happen as I took a break. What fears could get in my way? And what new ideas or direction might arise by giving myself space? If the book was meant to share the wisdom and process embedded within my maps, would time give me more maps, experiences and stories to share?

In this snippet of my map, showing just the specific leg about why my choice mattered, I let myself riff. Writing was new to me and I wanted to keep my process fun, not pressure-filled. I was curious to trust what it meant to listen as my intuition guided me to take a break. I wanted space to figure out how to best tell my stories.

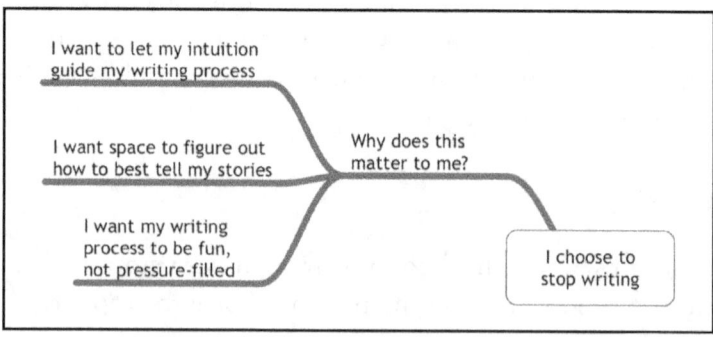

Having compassion for myself as I let my plans shift and owning my choice were challenging hurdles. It took courage to prevent myself from going down a guilt-filled rabbit hole. It took fortitude to squelch my inner critic, who so artfully and continually whispered my biggest fear—that if I stopped writing and sharing my message, my book would gather digital dust and I'd never do anything that mattered or make a real difference to those who needed my words. Instead, each morning, I had to find grace to stay hopeful and trust I'd know when it was time to begin writing again.

Present Choice 2

More than two years later, with the timing feeling right, I chose to start writing again and began a fresh present-day Exploration Map to examine why it mattered, my fears and the potential. Since much time had elapsed, I questioned how I'd find my way back to my message. Was the content still within me and did I have more to give? If I made time for my book, how might it affect my revenue-generating consulting work?

For this choice, I got clarity on why it mattered to me. (See the map at the top of the following page.) I believed my book would make a difference to many, it gave me great pleasure to speak about choice and I wanted to honor my promise to write this book.

I committed to the simple action of waking to write at 5 a.m.—no excuses. As I opened my computer, I reminded myself that I have a meaningful message to contribute and it's my deep desire to share it. Knowing I'd evolved since the book's first iteration, I wondered how I'd transcend my old words and bring the book into alignment with who I'd become during its hibernation.

I chose to show up each morning brave and faithful, tackling a sentence at a time, pulling apart thoughts, seeking the right words to convey my truth vulnerably and safely. Wanting to enjoy the process of writing, I chose to not focus on the finality of the book's ending, knowing the journey was as important as its completion. In retrospect, it's apparent that part of my book's path was to have breathing room to lay dormant.

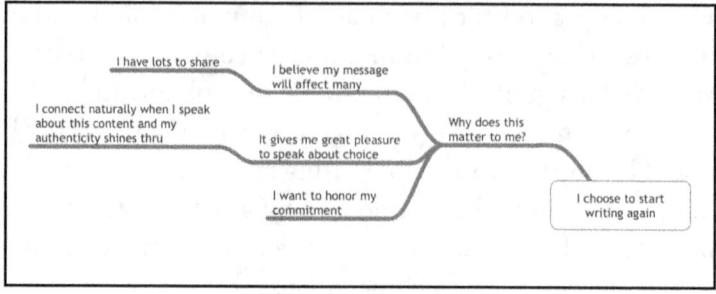

Present Choice 3

As a natural doer, choosing "not to do" is a big choice. A coach wisely shared that I'd gotten to where I was by doing, but to get where I dreamt of being I had to surrender and let go. Unplugging, turning off my electronics and not being available to anyone so I have space to think, sleep and be, not knowing what will come from being in that space, is not easy for me. My mind is rarely quiet and it's often easier to continue with my drug of doing than to surrender to silence. I question: What will come from space? What will I miss? What if no projects or money flow while I'm unplugged? What if I disappoint my clients because I'm not available? What if I become boring by "not doing", and then have to acknowledge that I work and stay busy because it's easier than having space? Does constant motion really signify accomplishment? What if, as Gandhi so wisely stated, speed is irrelevant if you're traveling in the wrong direction?

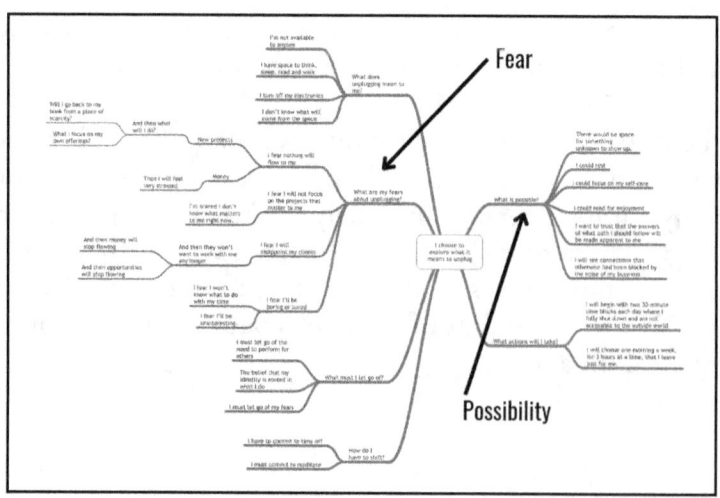

In the design of my *Unplugging Map*, I asserted my choice in the center: *I choose to explore what it means to unplug.* (Notice again that I incorporated the word "explore" in my statement to provide myself with spaciousness.)

I then captured why this choice mattered to me: I wanted to be inaccessible, having space to think, walk, read, and most importantly, I love the excitement of not knowing what will be birthed.

As I continued my questioning, building other branches of the map: What fears could get in my way of stepping into this choice? What was possible from this choice? I could see from their orientation on the page that, visually, the magnitude of fear on the left of the page mirrored the insidious thoughts swirling in my mind (see the image at the bottom of page 68). Seeing my thoughts so honestly mapped out made it very apparent that my fear was dwarfing what was possible, and it was imperative that for that reason alone I embark on the choice to unplug.

The reality that something as "simple" as unplugging was causing me so much angst was a blatant wake-up call illuminating why it was important that I take the requisite time daily to create space for myself. I don't want to live hostage to the fear of needing to perform for others, believing my identity is rooted in what I do.

Going through the exercise of exploring why this choice matters to me and getting to the bottom of my fears nudged me to build time into my schedule where I enforce shutting down. In unplugging there's stillness, and in the stillness there's possibility for something unknown to present itself. What new thoughts, ideas and connections may flow in that might otherwise be obstructed by the noise of busy-ness?

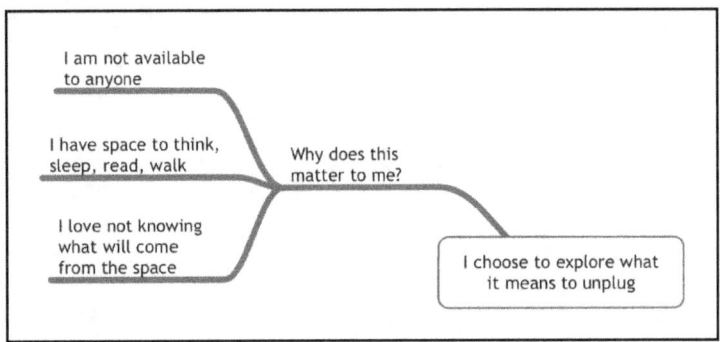

In each scenario, after clearly stating and owning my choice, I grounded into why it mattered at that moment. Investing time to create these maps kept the choice I was honoring at the forefront of my thoughts. Once I'd acknowledged my fears, which dissipated as the words filled the map's branches, I could address them with my adult brain. Putting the steps of each choice into a map allowed me to fully recognize the motivations behind them. This in turn empowered me to move forward with a clear understanding of exactly what I wanted to accomplish and how to do it.

CHAPTER 9

Professional Choices

In previous generations, the climb to a career destination was typically linear—a predictable move up the corporate ladder. Attend school, get a good job, get a promotion, continue working hard and then retire.

Today, non-linear career paths are the norm. While you may want stability, you likely also desire discovery and exploration. With evolving interests, meandering paths, ever-changing technology and unanticipated opportunities it's rare to follow a traditional model of career advancement. As Arianna Huffington shares, "Most people's careers zigzag and are full of unexpected moves and failures that lead to something better."

In the course of your career journey, you'll likely encounter one or more of the following **professional choices**:

- Will you leave your current job or embark upon a new career?
- Will you take time off or venture out on your own?
- Will you dedicate greater effort to what you're currently doing?

Once you've answered the primary Exploration Map question: *Why does this choice matter to you?*, your next step is to ask: **What fears could get in your way of stepping into this choice?**

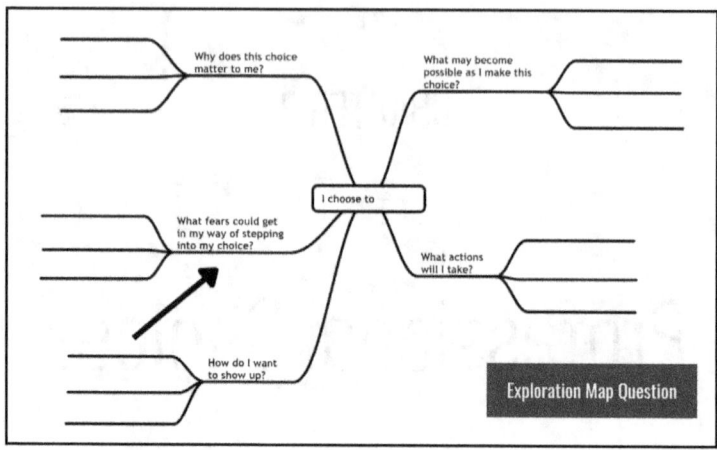

Whether you're choosing to change jobs, launch your own business or reinvent yourself, exposing your fears through honest inquiry and evaluating how to transcend them is a gift only you can give to yourself. Coaching yourself with effective questions will enable you to unearth information about what you want and what you fear that may have been previously inaccessible.

For a better understanding of how to answer this foundational Exploration Map question, let me share three scenarios where two clients and I confronted our fears directly. As you review these examples which utilize in-depth "what" questions, imagine yourself navigating similar situations and consider how you can apply them to circumstances you're currently facing.

Professional Choice 1

My client Kari reached out needing a "911 call" to express feeling overwhelmed with how hard she was pushing herself professionally. Hearing the pain in her voice, I asked what it would feel like to ease up and stop pushing. She softened as she contemplated my question, considering a choice she'd never let herself imagine.

Kari felt burdened by the weight of all she was doing and lived in perpetual fear that she'd fall behind if she didn't continue her relentless cycle of overextending herself. She approached every task with a frenetic sense of urgency that left her feeling exhausted.

Knowing she couldn't continue on the same path, Kari made a bold decision: *I choose to put all I'm doing on hold for one month and stop pressuring myself.*

Whenever Kari pushes, she tends to make decisions impulsively and unconsciously that affect her negatively because she's acting out of fear and anxiety. To stop beating herself up, she had to let go of the belief that she must control everything.

As we explored her choice, I focused on questions that provided insight into her cycle of overdoing.

"If you were to stop pushing and stop doing so much, what's at the root of all your fear?" I questioned.

"I've never been rejected—not from college or anything else I've ever applied for. This makes me wonder if I've not stretched myself. Did I not do enough or try hard enough?"

"When you consider not pushing for a short time, what scares you?" I asked.

"What if I miss an opportunity I'm supposed to have?" she answered.

"What if you did?" I inquired. "What would happen?"

"While I won't know what I missed, I fear another opportunity won't show up again. Even though my intellectual side knows this isn't true, my childlike self is nervous and anxious," she confided.

"Can you imagine how it'd feel to let go of the pressure of pushing?" I proposed.

Kari envisioned that she'd feel less exhausted, more peaceful and have a lighter sense of being.

As a final question, I asked, "What actions could you imagine taking to support yourself to become less driven?"

"I could imagine creating more space for being present and enjoying my life. I could also imagine meditating daily to quiet the incessant noise that reverberates in my head, pushing me."

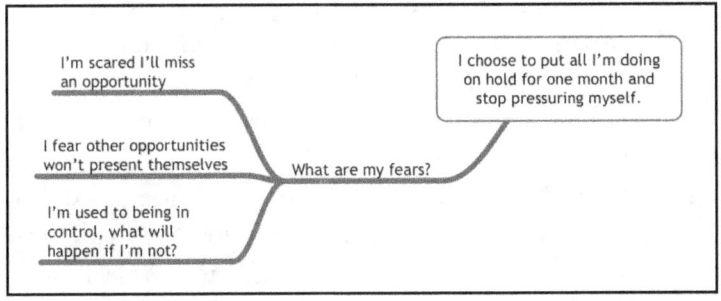

The unconscious mind's anxious prattling often stands in the way of change, steering us toward automatic, comfortable behaviors. Rather than making an empowered choice, it's natural to resume well-established habits and avoid taking actions that your intellect presumes will be daunting. Getting past your mind's rote thought-loops is critical for meaningful shifts to occur.

Professional Choice 2

Shortly after beginning to write this book, I decided to shut down my *Get It Done U* business website. When I first launched my virtual storefront, I focused on perfecting each offering that taught entrepreneurs how to get things done. As my fascination for exploring choices and creating maps developed, I wanted to concentrate on the wide range of ideas and opportunities that emerged from my book-writing process. I'd stopped devoting attention to my business and it felt disconcerting to have an online presence that wasn't in alignment with where my energy was directed.

Wanting to embrace the belief that for the new to enter I must release the old, I considered walking away from a business I'd built over eight years. This intention exposed many fears: Who would I be without my prior business identity? Would anyone find me without any visible credibility of my accomplishments? Would all the years I'd spent creating have been for naught? Would I end up financially destitute without this source of income?

Using an Exploration Map, I made sense of my answers.

Those doubts echoed the concerned questions my father asked me when I left my first stable job in my twenties for a startup. Back then, I responded, "If this next opportunity doesn't work, I'm built on a solid foundation and I'll be fine." Recalling those words, I understood that I needed to adopt a similar response in my fifties. I had to trust that my prior steps were necessary for my evolution, and that freeing myself from past encumbrances would allow me to fully step into my next incarnation.

After weeks of deliberation, I chose to dismantle my website and release my prior business identity. Shutting down provided me with space to focus my efforts on high-end consulting projects so I could earn an income while I wrote. More importantly, it marked my choice to forge an identity as a thought leader versus how effective I am at getting things done. Letting go nudged me to live the principles I share in this book and trust in my own unfolding.

Once I addressed my fears about closing down my site and took action to write, my confidence grew and my optimism blossomed. As a result of this choice, my trust deepened that my book would serve as a beacon guiding others to learn more about my life's work.

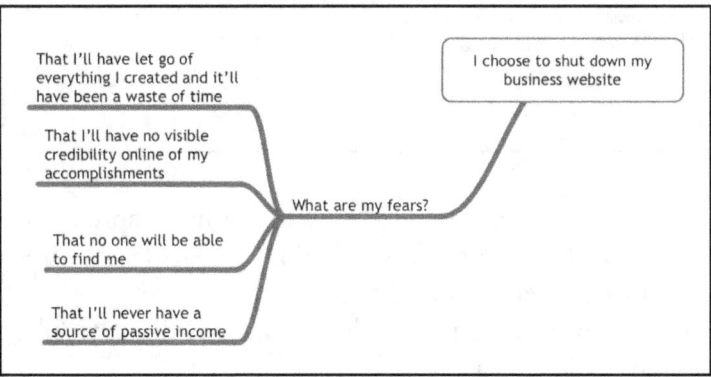

Professional Choice 3

When you yearn for something in the distance, but notice that you remain stuck where you are, ask yourself honestly what is blocking you.

As a motivational speaker, Jai was ready to share her work more publicly and stated her choice clearly: *I choose to share my gifts and do whatever it takes to do that.*

"What fears could hold you back from stepping into this choice?" I inquired.

Her list was long.

- She feared others wouldn't show up and listen to her.
- Afraid they wouldn't like her, or her message, she questioned her ability to communicate clearly.
- She feared she'd stay mediocre.
- If she revealed her ideas honestly, she was concerned that her audience might be offended.
- She agonized over her belief that she didn't have the technical knowledge she needed.

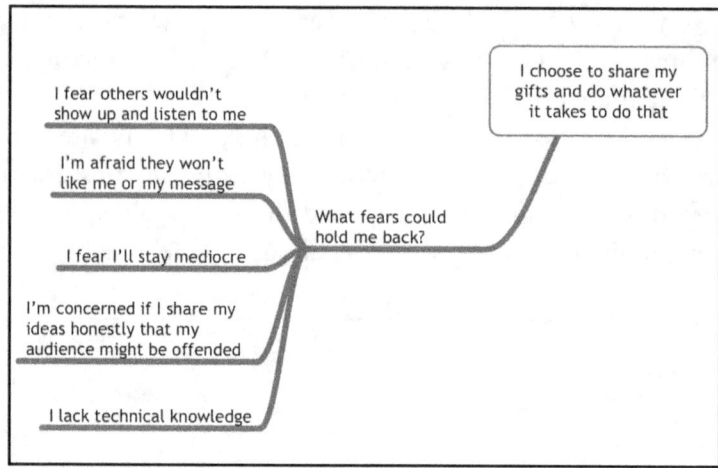

As she verbalized her fears, which were firmly anchored to her past, the heaviness in her energy was palpable. She had to address them unequivocally in order to move beyond them.

"Some of your fears sound outdated," I stated directly, "like they're rooted in old stories. Is that possible?"

"Of course, it's possible; I hadn't thought about that."

Wanting to determine how "live" each of her fears actually was, I took her through a quick gut-check exercise.

"Let's examine your fear of others not liking you—is that really true? You're a grown woman with three children. Are you anxious that some random person you don't know won't like you? Is that an irrational fear or does it still have a hold on you? From 1 to 10, what would you give it?"

"You're right; that one's reflective of a younger version of me. I used to be a big people-pleaser, but I've evolved and learned to deal with negative feedback. I'd say that's a 2. Give me another one," she excitedly requested.

"What about the fear that you're going to stay mediocre?"

"That's not true any longer. At this point, I'd depress myself if I didn't shine as brightly as I know I can. That one's probably a 3."

I pointed out that her first two fears were rooted in old stories. She discovered as she dug deeper and challenged these narratives that she wasn't as held back as she'd allowed herself to believe. Questioning these automatic thoughts defused their emotional power and enabled her to build a new, more truthful story about what she needed to do to see her choice through.

"Tell me about your fear of not knowing the technology piece."

"That's still a big one for me. When I think about all the technology needed to create my website, I become overwhelmed. I don't know how to do it, and don't want to learn."

"What about hiring it out?" I proposed. "No one said you must do everything yourself. Your gift is your message, not your technical prowess."

"I know, but I'm scared of spending money."

"I get that, but what about looking at it another way?" I suggested. "Without putting your work out in the world in a way that other people can digest, you'll never be able to receive money. How about finding a reasonably priced virtual assistant to help with some of the more challenging tasks that will ultimately lead to revenue?"

"I know you're right, I've just been resistant."

"So, what will it take for you to own that you don't need to be the chief cook in your business and let go of certain tasks that are not your strengths?

"Clearly it's time, I just have to do it."

When you've had a challenging professional experience, it's natural to feel unnerved and question how you got yourself into that situation. An involuntary response is to judge yourself, your skills and your behavior, asking, *what's wrong with me?* This query, with its underlying judgmental tone, leaves you feeling victimized and mired in negative emotions. To be more supportive of yourself, consider shifting your question to, *what lessons can I glean from what happened so I can make better decisions in the future?*

Let me share with you an example I'm sure you can relate to. Think back to a time when you felt demoralized because of an uncomfortable situation with a boss. Despite the fact that your boss was probably as bad as you remember, what if, rather than blaming them, you made a more constructive choice? For instance, *I choose to move on from this uncomfortable professional experience.*

Using inquiry to examine a less-than-savory experience with openness and fearlessness allows you to garner meaningful insights so you don't drag negativity into your future. Every drama has two sides, and regardless of how bad you felt and how angry you were, imagine looking at your actions and attitude with profound vulnerability and wise candor so you can assume responsibility and evolve from your experience.

Admitting the truth of how you showed up, what you didn't do well and what you could do better affords you the ability to unveil your shortcomings and identify avenues for personal and professional growth. Positive aspects are often found in even the most challenging circumstances.

Creating an Exploration Map to process a tough experience with an eye to insight rather than resentment is an opportunity for personal development. By combing through the archives of your professional choices, you may see evidence of dated narratives and recurring patterns you continue to repeat in spite of your fervent wish that the future take a different trajectory. By looking within, you can address your fears, gain clarity about what's important to you and conduct yourself with confidence. Breaking from repetitive and monotonous cycles requires owning your part and asking honest questions that lead you to a place where you can learn and affect change.

As you self-reflect, consider asking yourself these powerful questions to gain a new perspective:

- What can you do to support yourself to not run from confrontation and challenging personalities?

- What specific aspects of this dynamic would you like to avoid replicating?

- To avoid holding on to old baggage, what honest conversations must you have with yourself?

- What wisdom can you draw from this experience to carry forth into the future?

- As you handle challenging predicaments, what resources can you draw upon to cope?

As you face making present-day professional choices, become curious, pose powerful questions and follow the threads of your answers. Asking yourself thoughtful questions unlocks a sense of lightness and possibility, helping you to better understand what you want before feeling the pressure to find your way to a definitive choice.

CHAPTER 10

Relationship Choices

As you make **relationship choices** you're focusing on whether to begin a new relationship, work on mending, supporting or building one you're already in or end one that's no longer fulfilling.

Relationship choices are often highly charged and it can feel as though the weight of your future rests on the decision to stay or go.

- Will you choose to work on a relationship you're already in and address its challenges?

- Will you choose to stay with intention or let the relationship wane?

- Will you choose to end a relationship that no longer meets your needs?

- Will you embark upon a new relationship?

- Will you reconnect to someone who's mattered to you?

Before we dive into the various relationship choices, let's take a closer look at the third Exploration Map question which will serve as the lens through which we view these choices: ***How do you want to show up as you make your choice?***

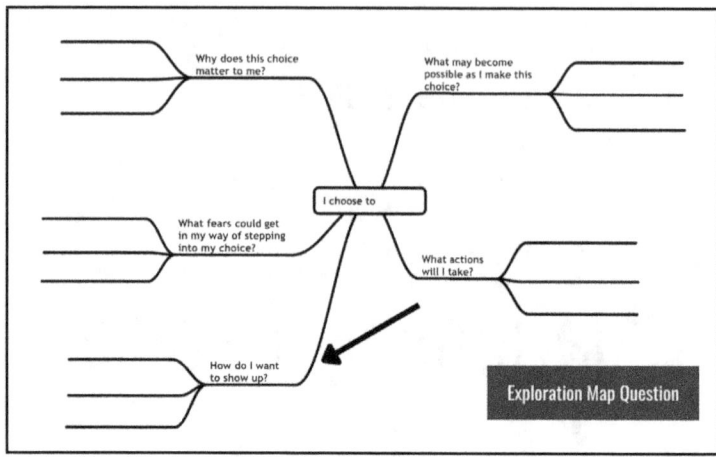

To access wisdom around your relationships, it's beneficial to approach them from the perspective of how you're showing up. This question encourages you to reflect on your interpersonal dynamics and your role in the relationship. As it's paramount to reflect on this question, I've highlighted this section to emphasize its importance.

Focus on How You're Showing Up

At the crossroads of a new choice, regardless of how you've conducted yourself in the past, you have the ability to embrace attributes that are important to you and step into being the person you want to be. With each new person who enters your life, you have the opportunity to shape how you'll show up in the relationship.

What might be possible when you step into your values, making them come to life with intentional action? What part of you might be set free when you take responsibility for clumsy actions? What connection and intimacy might be available to you when you address underlying relationship tensions so you can speak more honestly?

As you consider how to apply this question of how you're showing up to a choice you're making, take a moment to-bring to mind someone in your life where you're feeling a disconnection—maybe it's your partner, your child or your mother. The rift might be due to an action that occurred, a story you've created or something underlying that's getting in the way of the relationship being where you want it to be. With the goal of finding your way back to them, consider the following questions that support you to address how you're showing up:

- Where can you take responsibility?
- What can you do to show up differently?
- Where can you be kinder and more compassionate?
- What can you stop and start doing?
- What will it take for you to listen with a more open heart?
- What's the cost to both of you by not making this effort?

Each person you allow into your inner sphere has influence and power, and the choices you make in your interactions mold your relationships over time. After an unpleasant interaction, it's not uncommon to think that sidestepping the discomfort of a challenging conversation is the best answer. What if instead, as an alternative, you committed to taking complete responsibility for what you've said or done when things go awry?

If you've previously crossed a line or overstepped a boundary, you can, in present time, consciously choose to overcome your embarrassment, own your actions and apologize sincerely. How you've reacted to slights, how you've handled mistakes and whether you've reached out when you were unsure of what to say, each exemplify how you showed up.

When you haven't handled a situation in a manner that leaves you feeling good about yourself, you have the choice to do it differently in your next interaction.

Focusing on how you want to show up, and getting intentional about listening to your heart has the potential to add a rich dimension to your decision-making process. As you engage in challenging and uncomfortable conversations, commit to showing up impeccably and bringing great consciousness to the words you speak.

The following questions take your thinking to a deeper level related to how you're showing up, so your relationship has greater potential to flourish and evolve. Your responses will allow you to own your role and more clearly understand what is required for your interactions to improve.

- What might transform in your dynamic as you speak truthful words, even when the truthful words are difficult to utter?

- What would you need to be able to do, including seeking support, to move from communicating what is polite and on the surface, to being more vulnerable and direct?

- What would those words of confrontation, ownership and expression be?

- What shifts can you make in how you speak and interact?

Consider how different your actions might look as you choose to show up impeccably in your relationships, bringing awareness to speaking your truth. Speaking with honesty allows you to show up transparently and bring healing to a relationship that matters to you.

Opportunities to bring awareness to how you show up present themselves in significant moments, as well as in the ordinary and mundane. As you become more agile at utilizing this particular Exploration Map question, you'll become adept at applying it in the moment as you're out and about in your life, without a map.

While writing this book, I've developed a sensitivity to real-time scenarios where I must critically confront the question of how I am showing up versus how I'd prefer to show up. As I shift from teacher to student, employing the concepts I'm sharing with you, I call upon valuable insights I've gathered. I've had situations where it's clear I must reframe my thinking, adjust my actions and prevent myself from relying on behaviors I know don't serve me. I then seek the root of what I'm feeling so I can speak more truthfully and demonstrate respect for the person I'm in relationship with.

In one scenario, my partner and I were having guests over for lunch and I'd asked him to pick up a few ingredients on his way home from a meeting. Opening the door to see me cooking, he immediately remembered he'd forgotten what he was supposed to get and critiqued his absent-mindedness.

While a small flash of annoyance flickered through my thoughts, I prevented myself from adding to his anguish. Was it really a big deal? Did I need to belabor the point and make him feel bad?

What if instead, with a small change in my behavior, I could shift our dynamic?

Noticing he was caught in the messiness and guilt of his thoughts, I chose to diffuse the situation and show up with kindness. I took his face into my hands, looked into his eyes, let him know I wasn't upset and asked him to shake it off. Lunch would go on.

In another instance, while taking a trail walk he shared that he'd overlooked doing something I asked him to do. In the silence of our ensuing steps, he moved into his well-worn story of feeling inadequate for being forgetful and I moved into mine that I would take care of it myself, as I always do.

As twigs crunched beneath my feet, I felt the nudge to heed the guidance of my own advice.

Kim, what would it take for you to choose to show up as you want to be, I thought to myself. *To stop berating and silently stewing, to release drama, to not go down an unnecessarily dark and un-communicative road? Can you reframe your perspective and see him as a human who forgot versus being an unreliable man who cannot be depended upon?*

Observing the situation from a different vantage point, I softened. Not wanting to act childlike and victimized, spiraling into added drama, I consciously chose to let my anger go. This shift allowed us to have the conversation which lay beneath the surface, beyond the significance of one forgotten task. I chose language that allowed me to share the truth of my feelings and express my frustration, while not making him feel worse. We continued to walk through the woods, our steps falling into sync. Focusing on how I wanted to show up let us proceed together instead of getting mired in old stories and walking alone.

On a crowded, rush hour train leaving the city on a Friday night, I placed my bag on the vacant seat beside me to save it for a friend. As miffed passengers eyed my bag with irritation, I felt pressure to relinquish the spot.

"Is this seat free?" a harried traveler questioned.

"No, I'm waiting for my friend," I retorted.

"Come on," she whined, "the train's leaving in a minute. Let me sit down and if she gets here, I'll move."

Begrudgingly I grabbed my bag to give her space and put my headphones on to display my disdain.

As the train departed, with my friend nowhere in sight, the woman dropped her purse. Feeling a strong desire to connect with a stranger I'd treated contemptuously, I removed the self-imposed barrier of my headphones, reached for her purse and established eye contact as I handed it to her as a peace offering. She warmed.

"I'm sorry for acting so bitchy," I apologized. "I was hoping to spend time with my friend and I'm disappointed she missed the train."

"I get it but I would have moved if she'd gotten here."

"I know, but I'm still sorry for how I acted. I was unnecessarily obnoxious."

"Thank you for saying that," she said.

And in the brevity of a moment the tension between us dissipated, and we each returned to our private space.

By taking the time within that "small" moment to examine how I was showing up, I was able to forge a positive human connection where before I had allowed negative energy to define the experience.

The ability to bring heightened awareness to how you show up in your relationships can be extremely beneficial. As we continue in this section, we'll explore a breadth of relationship choices through the lens of the question: **How do you want to show up as you make your choice?**

Relationship Choice 1

We are in relationships with people we invite into our lives who matter to us—romantic partners, blood relatives and friends who become our chosen family. And, until we make a conscious choice to change, we are also in relationship with those we are better served to be without. Change happens when we mindfully face the challenging and uncomfortable moments encountered in our relationships. Taking the perspective of *how you want to show up* can make this huge task more manageable.

Some toxic relationships, imbued with negative energy, are challenging to renounce. An undercurrent of guilt as well as the cultural stigma of walking away, can prevent us from making what we know is likely the healthiest choice. While you may not entirely believe this, whether you maintain a relationship with someone is always under your control.

"It's a sad and hard choice to let people go," my dear friend, Mia, poignantly shared after having made the difficult choice to disconnect and lessen communication with her older brother. He'd been her person for years. He understood the pain she experienced with their mentally unstable mother and controlling sister in a way no one else could.

That said, as he dealt with the angst and guilt of his alcoholic son's disruptive behavior, he began having volatile outbursts and treating Mia badly. While she understood the pressures he was experiencing and wished she could forgive him for lashing out, she chose to stop subjecting herself to his explosive and increasingly abusive conduct.

"No matter how much you love someone," she shared, "there's a breaking point when it's too painful to continue. I had to stop hoping he'd be different. He was so immersed in his hurt that he'd lost sight of who I was, and he spoke abusively and condescendingly to me as if I were a stranger."

How, she asked herself, did she want to show up in her relationship with her brother?

Mia chose to set clear boundaries to protect herself. While she allowed for sporadic conversations, she invested little of her emotional energy and maintained low expectations. Years of unmet hopes forced her to assert that she would not continue to invest in relationships that are draining and hurtful.

Documenting her clear words within her Exploration Map, provided Mia with a resource to recall her commitment: she would no longer enable his bad behavior, she would set clear boundaries and she would be kind, yet strong.

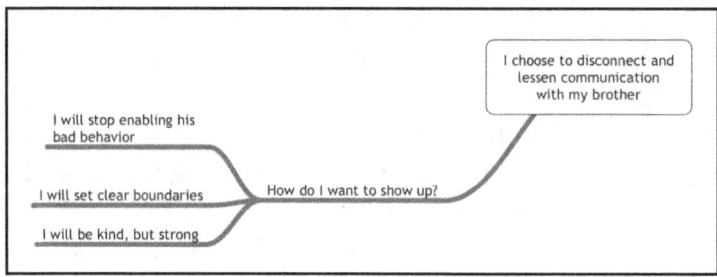

- Like Mia, where in your life might you have an opportunity to take a stand for yourself?
- Where can you clean up a relationship that is not serving you, is weighing you down and is not in your highest good?
- Where can you shift a dynamic by changing how you show up?

Relationship Choice 2

Each day you have the opportunity to choose who you will attend to and cherish, and in which relationships you invest your energy.

When you're in an unhealthy relationship, you have the choice to either make it work or not. It's a time of responsibility and reckoning. Relationships require love and care to thrive—it's your choice which relationships you nurture and invest in, and which you don't. You choose daily who you let into your life, and to what extent.

When you're feeling detached from someone who matters to you—a romantic partner, friend, parent, business partner or sibling—making the choice to find your way back allows for your reconnection.

Sarah, a college-aged client, felt despair because of the estranged relationship she had with her father. As she contemplated finding her way back to him, she questioned: Did it matter, was it worth it, did she care?

As a young adult she didn't feel she had the emotional maturity to answer these weighty questions, but the stagnancy of indecision and immobility plagued her. I suggested she focus on making the "small" choice to have one interaction and tolerate the uncertainty of what would come next, trusting if she moved slowly, she could handle what showed up.

Her choice to initiate one interaction was an opening of a door, an extension of an olive branch, a subtle but definitive statement that this relationship mattered to her. When she shared that she didn't yet have the words to express what was in her heart, I suggested she have patience with herself. Her only choice at this moment was to open the door to the possibility of a renewed relationship. She did not have to walk the balance of the path all at once, there was time in the future for those steps to become clearer.

The piece she could control, which was how she showed up, meant being hopeful and open to the possibility of a reconciliation. While her fears were primarily related to uncertainty, she sought to trust that with support she could handle whatever arose. Returning to the powerful statements in her map became an anchor when she felt unmoored and off-kilter, aiding her to find her footing.

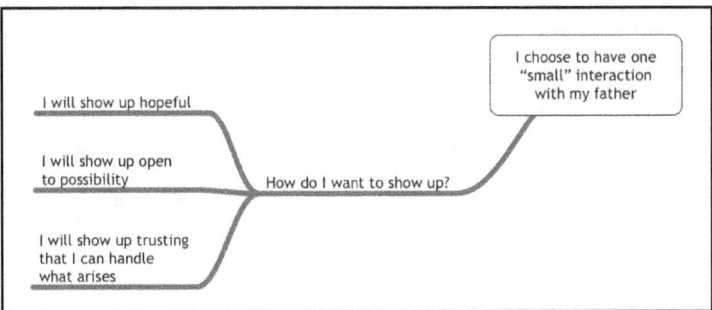

Relationship Choice 3

Approaching relationship decisions consciously is a daily practice, a choice of recommitment. In any moment, even in the small moments, you have the ability to pivot and take responsibility for how your actions affect others. Being fully present can reveal untapped reserves of emotion, capability and strength that might not have emerged otherwise.

When my client Eva's friend and patient was diagnosed with a third round of cancer, she fell into a self-destructive behavior of avoiding her calls. Knowing she couldn't be the healer she wished she could, Eva withdrew, not feeling equipped to connect effectively in this emotionally grueling situation. The guilt she felt was exacerbated by the shame she carried from avoiding two other sick friends years earlier.

As we spoke of her dilemma, I gently asked, "Regardless of how you acted before, how would you like to show up now?"

Despite wanting to be there for her friend, Eva dreaded their conversation. Deep in her gut she knew her friend was dying, but hearing the words definitively stated would expose a truth she wasn't prepared to accept. Would magical thinking and avoiding their conversation postpone the inevitable?

Sensing a question she'd not considered, I asked, "What would it feel like to show up in the honesty of what's going on for you? Can you imagine explaining that you're feeling inadequate in your inability to heal her, but want to be there in the truth of whatever she's experiencing?"

Considering my questions, Eva knew it was important that she show up with the compassion, presence and openness her friend deserved. The simplicity of honoring how she pledged to show up served as a touchstone, a reminder that she could embody the qualities that matter to her, no longer hiding and behaving negligently as she had in the past.

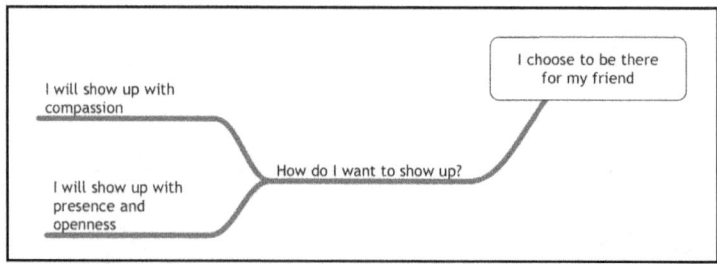

You are in a relationship because it brings value into your life and what emerges from that relationship is formed by the energy and commitment you invest. Regardless of the depth of your bond, in any relationship that matters, you can be conscientious in acting in accordance with your highest ideals, even if you haven't done this in the past. As the examples in this chapter illustrate, subtle shifts in how you choose to show up have the power to change your challenging dynamics, positively or negatively. You can't force a specific outcome, but you can embody the qualities you value as you communicate despite difficult circumstances.

CHAPTER 11

Reactive Choices

While the focus of Part 3 has been on the proactive choices we make, there are times we make reactive choices.

Your reactive choices are those you make in response to something external that's happened to you, something you did not choose for yourself.

Your partner leaves you. You get sick. Something happens with your child. You get fired. The thing that mattered to you didn't happen the way you envisioned. A situation arises that you didn't plan for. Someone makes a choice on your behalf.

During these distressing moments, a less-than-perfect circumstance is forced upon you. These situations can be disorienting and feel awful, especially because they're not something you've chosen for yourself.

In the space of a reactive choice, it's natural to believe that you're a victim who's not in control—that people are doing things to you, and that life is unfairly handing you challenges. However, even in the context of an unanticipated, ceiling-crashing-down moment you aren't stripped of your power. The way you react, respond and show up is always up to you.

Reactive situations often require you to respond quickly, in the moment. In the limited time you have, it helps to approach this in the same way as relationship choices: *How do I want to show up?* In the following section, I share two personal examples where I let this question guide my dialogue around reactive choice.

Reactive Choice 1

I was in a small mastermind coaching group led by a woman I greatly admired. To support one of the women in our group who was newer to coaching I agreed to step in as her client to provide her with an opportunity to practice her coaching skills. Not knowing what to expect, I was pleasantly surprised during our first session to discover the many strengths she had to support me and I began to anticipate our upcoming coaching sessions with excitement. A month into working together, she shared that the leader of our mastermind no longer wanted her to coach anyone in our small group and she would need to end our coaching.

"How do you feel?" she inquired.

"I feel like I have no choice in the matter. I feel like the decision was made for me. I feel like big brother swooped in."

Wanting to understand our mastermind leader, I sat with my percolating emotions, wondering what would cause her to make such a dictatorial directive. Though I had hoped to feel empathy, anger was what bubbled to the surface. Choosing to address this situation directly, I reached out to ask why she'd made her unilateral decision.

She shared her fears of losing her livelihood as my new coach began encroaching on her professional territory. While I understood her concerns and feelings of scarcity, I questioned why she'd made her demand without consulting me privately. Asking if my new coaching relationship mattered to me would have allowed for an alternative plan that served each of us.

She apologized, explaining she'd had a dark night of the soul moment and was confronting personal truths that were painful to acknowledge. She requested I view her with compassion and accept her human foibles. While able to accommodate her request, I internally questioned if continuing in the mastermind was my best choice, knowing I could only stay if I felt confident I could open myself to receive her coaching support in our group.

The following day she shared a message with humble words, "Thank you for your courage and for caring enough to confront me over our recent situation. You could have walked away."

Walking away would have been the easy choice, the choice without confrontation, the choice where I could make her wrong, the choice where I could stay in the victim's role because something was done to me.

Instead, after having developed deeper awareness and taken the many steps needed to reconnect with important people in my life, I chose to find my way back to my coach. My choice, and how we honestly communicated about what occurred, paved the way for our relationship to deepen and for me to continue to thrive in our mastermind group.

Reactive Choice 2

Recognizing potential victim-like emotions allows you to manage your negative energy. Rather than asking why something happened *to* you, consider asking why it happened *for* you. Why may this choice be happening for your highest good? This subtle reframe allows you to shift from the lower vibrational energy of the victim into using your wise mind, trusting that buried under the muck of what's happened is your ability to proactively choose how you'll respond, how you'll show up and how you'll move forward.

For a fun summer project when my son Beck was fifteen, I bought him a course to teach him to sell information and products online. When he got to the module focused on choosing his domain name, I suggested that he reach out to his dad to get some marketing direction.

After picking him up from baseball, I asked, "How'd it go choosing a domain with dad?"

"He said the whole thing we're doing is stupid and he won't invest in a domain for something he thinks is a scam. He asked why I was learning from you when you've never been a success at anything you've ever done."

I gasped. In the presence of my son, in the close confines of our SUV, I felt sucker-punched and deeply embarrassed. Did Allan really voice such hideous thoughts about me? I felt angry and humiliated as Beck repeated these words, but summoned the strongest version of myself to regain my footing.

The following day I reached out to a spiritual friend asking how I could shift to a healthier and more evolved space after hearing Allan's harsh and degrading words.

"I know you're feeling venom toward your ex and want to lash out," my spiritual friend stated with incredible clarity, "but for your own growth, can you consider seeing him as a loving messenger? His words pierced your heart, but understand that they only impacted you because you believe they carry truth. Consider for a moment that he's an important spiritual guide, and his purpose in your life is to point you to a lesson you're ready to learn. Would you be willing to see this humiliating situation differently and love him for being your messenger? If you can open your heart to seeing what happened in a new light, it may enable you to release your negative energy."

I was caught between worlds: the ordinary world where my friend's point of view felt like idiotic woo nonsense, and the more evolved spiritual world where I wanted to embrace and love Allan for communicating a charged message that exposed my vulnerable limiting belief.

I had often questioned the definition of what made me a success and spent many therapy sessions delving into issues around my self-worth. My truth was that I didn't feel like a success. If I had, Allan's words would have bounced off, never penetrating my inner core.

After weeks of straddling two worlds, I chose to focus on discerning why this experience happened *for* me, not *to* me. Allan's message was a prompt that I needed to resume the work I'd begun in therapy.

Addressing the pain caused by my reaction to his comments, I moved into my trusty "what" questions and asked myself the following:

- What story am I telling myself based on his words?
- What truth can I acknowledge in what he's shared?
- What new definition of success can I create that feels authentic for me?
- What will it take for me to let go of the pain of his words?

When others' decisions are foisted upon you, you can choose to respond in a manner that restores your strength and extricates you from the victim's role. Even when you're not the driver of the situation, you're always in charge of your ability to make a new, proactive choice about how to proceed. As Maya Angelou beautifully shares, "You may not control all the events that happen to you, but you can decide not to be reduced by them."

You can choose to feel angry, victimized and vengeful, or you can choose to be trusting, hopeful and grateful. While you may not have a choice about whether or not you will experience a challenge or obstacle, you always have the ability to choose how you'll show up should you find yourself in a moment of crisis.

With conscious thought and a strong resolve, you can own what's negative and choose to alchemize it into more supportive feelings, and from there into meaningful and purposeful action.

CHAPTER 12

Personal Choices

Proactive choices are those you make consciously to move toward something that matters to you. Thus far, we've covered two categories of present-day, proactive choices—those you make professionally and those you make in relationships. We've also looked at reactive choices, which are those made in response to something that's happened outside of your control.

In this section we'll cover the final category of proactive choice which are your personal choices.

Your personal choices involve bringing something into your life that matters, or letting go of something that doesn't. You may choose to move, embrace a new opportunity, write a book or cultivate more joy in your life. As you seek growth and development, you may want to heal from past wounds and work with a therapist.

Making a personal choice is a powerful springboard to orient your life in a direction that has meaning—to step into what you trust is in your best interest and remain faithful and confident that you're moving toward something that's right for you. When you bring consciousness to making choices from the perspective of what matters, you can trust you've made the best choice possible at that moment.

You may be choosing to say yes or no to an opportunity. You may be choosing to do something that supports your personal growth—asking for what you want, taking a stand for yourself or taking a deeper look at what triggers you. You may be choosing to shift your attitude to feel more gratitude, more joy, more openness.

Personal choices of all sizes and complexities are a chance to affirm what matters.

Here are some broad examples of personal choices:

- Choosing to make an uncomfortable choice
- Choosing to make a loving choice
- Choosing to bring joy into your life
- Choosing to do something that scares you
- Choosing to learn something new
- Choosing to focus on your self-care
- Choosing to teach something
- Choosing to let go of something that no longer serves you

As we move into our exploration of personal choices, we'll look at the questions you're asking about choices through the lens of intuition—the indispensable and ever-present guide at your disposal, there to act as your North Star.

When you're on the brink of making a new choice, you may think you need to have it all figured out, to know where you're heading and to have a plan. You may question why your choice even matters to you.

As you consider a choice, you may call upon your analytical brain to find facts and data, or tap into your gut feelings and intuition. Whether you lean more heavily on one of these styles or use them together, learning to turn inward to trust your internal voice provides you access to your most innate asset, your omnipresent guide.

To best connect with the wisdom of your gut as your internal compass and trust it as a viable resource, you'll benefit from looking back and reflecting on how you've been guided so far. You can then apply your insights to hone your instincts to make better decisions going forward.

Messages and signs often come in whispers. When you're not tuned in, or your head's full of noise, you may miss the subtle nudge of your inner voice, forcing your body to speak louder and more insistently. Allowing for quiet in your daily life affords you the ability to hear the faint murmurs and choose to take action, or not. Bringing quiet into your life is paramount so you can listen and notice all that your inner wisdom has to share.

Each of us possesses this knowing of what's best for us. First, you have to choose to listen. Then, you must listen with openness to what you're hearing. By building the muscle of listening you become more adept at using it, and over time the muscle grows stronger.

Previously, we used the first three Exploration Map questions as filters through which to look at your choices.

1. Why does this choice matter to you? (Chapter 8)

2. What fears might get in your way of stepping into your choice? (Chapter 9)

3. How do you want to show up as you make your decision? (Chapter 10)

In this chapter, I'll guide and orient you to using your intuition as another part of your process. For some, making a choice is analytical and rational; for others it's intuitive and visceral. Often, it's a blend of both.

Personal Choice 1

To tap into the wisdom of your gut and trust it as a viable resource, you need practice making decisions and assessing what you've learned and experienced from your past choices. Exercising your intuition allows you to hone your instincts in order to make better choices moving forward.

When my youngest son was in eighth grade, I invited him to make his first conscious, intentional choice, giving him a baseline experience to build his intuition. Sensing he might enjoy and excel in a hands-on learning environment, I presented him with two academic options: the large, well-respected, public high school his friends would attend or the smaller, experiential magnet school where he'd have to make new friendships. Although I wasn't attached to which school he chose, I encouraged him to take the exploration and interview process seriously, enabling him to make the best decision for himself.

With each step of the magnet school's group walk-through, private interview and shadow day, we spoke about the pros and cons of each option. Rather than using his logical brain to make this decision, I suggested he tap into his gut, a tool he had no experience using.

"Regardless of logic," I asked him, "which choice feels best to you?"

While he appreciated the smaller school's offerings, he had an internal hunch that the larger public school would better meet his needs. Even though he landed in the same place he would have had he not done this exercise, he'd made an intentional choice rather than following the crowd. At fourteen, he experienced making his first life-defining choice, one based on gut instinct, and established a baseline from which to develop his intuitive muscle.

Personal Choice 2

Danna, a single woman in her forties, discovered she carried the BRCA2 gene, putting her at an increased risk of developing breast cancer. Although she was fortunate to have a clean cancer screening, she had a choice to make. Would she prophylactically remove her breasts and undergo reconstruction? Would she opt out of surgery but continue to get screened more frequently? Would she send her body into early menopause by removing her ovaries, but not her breasts, which would reduce her risk of breast cancer by 50%?

Having a guide in her cousin, who'd wrestled with similar questions months earlier, Danna did her medical due diligence and consulted with both Eastern and Western practitioners. Having no cancer in her system and not wanting to risk it occurring, she chose to undergo radical surgery and remove her breasts and ovaries in one long surgical day.

"Of all the information you received," I questioned, "what supported you to make your choice?"

"I had a strong inner knowing of what was right for me. As someone who gets stressed easily and doesn't handle uncertainty well, I wanted to keep my anxiety at bay. Without surgery, I would have been plagued by daily low-grade worrying, unnecessary suspense and stress before each yearly screening."

Danna gathered facts and information, spoke to a variety of professionals to understand her options and felt into what was right for her. By combining her intuition with a methodical list, she reached the decision she felt best about. And once she made her choice, she was unwavering.

Your strong instinct doesn't have to be complicated or require a huge epiphany. It's an internal sense, a visceral beat, a deep knowledge of self, a feeling of wanting to move forward. Once you recognize your knowing, you're able to make a choice and take action to honor it.

Personal Choice 3

Trusting your instincts is challenging, especially when external voices seem louder than your own.

My close friend, Amy, faced a heart-wrenching decision about whether to put her dog Rocket to sleep after his health deteriorated and he wasn't living a quality life. Rocket was like a child to Amy, and it devastated her when she considered this choice.

Despite Amy's gut telling her that euthanizing Rocket was in the dog's best interest, the vet's questioning of her motivation prompted her logical brain to second guess this decision.

Although Amy used her gut instinct as a guide, she still questioned whether she'd made the right decision. From my vantage point, I explained that her choice honored what mattered to her, which was for Rocket to leave this earth feeling safe, loved and peaceful.

Choices are often framed with "right" and "wrong" language, infusing them with guilt, judgment and heaviness.

In speaking with Amy, I reassured her by saying, "You made the best choice you could after considering all your options and most importantly, considering your love for Rocket. It may be hard, but can you trust that you brought all your heart to your choice and it's the best one to have made?"

It's paramount to approach your meaningful choices with reverence, allowing your options to percolate. When considering how to best honor your values, listen to your inner voice for guidance. Call upon your internal and external resources—those of your internal navigation system, your logical brain and the brains of others. By infusing your choice-making with a consciousness to what matters, you'll feel greater confidence that you're making the best decision you can in the moment.

As we come to the end of Part 3 about Present Choices, we've explored three of the key Exploration Map questions. If you want a refresher on these questions, you'll find a guide to their chapter locations in the table below.

Exploration Map Questions We've Covered So Far	Chapter
Why does this choice matter to you?	8
What fears could get in your way of stepping into your choice?	9
How do you want to show up as you make your choice?	10

PART 4

Past Choices
Accepting How You Got Where You Are

You Can't Go Back
And Change the Beginning
But
You Can Start Where You Are
And Change The Ending
—C.S. Lewis

CHAPTER 13

No Wrong Choices

When recalling a past choice, our minds naturally sort them into two categories: the "bad ones" we regret, and the "good ones" we view with pride and appreciation. The emotional charge attached to our "bad" choices often impedes us from delving into how and why we made those choices, and ultimately how we handled their fallout.

While it's natural to want to avoid uncovering elements of your past that you might prefer to keep hidden, owning the truth of your past choices' consequences and looking back with objectivity empowers you to take full responsibility for all that you expose within the shadowy recesses of a choice.

In choosing to own where you've been, and by looking at what you did and what you learned, you're able to bring greater consciousness and thoughtfulness to making healthier future choices.

Examining past choices can be uncomfortable because it's likely you didn't make each one from the highest, purest place—a nearly impossible task within the human experience. While you may feel shame and regret when you look at these choices and your subsequent actions, your unbiased reflection has the potential to furnish you with insight about who you were and why you did what you did.

What if no choice you made, or could make, was ever wrong? What if each choice was in your highest good because of the lessons you learned and how it set you up to make better choices going forward?

We typically go through life making decisions in our head, alone, rarely making time to appreciate the impact of each choice. Whether a particular choice was the best decision of your life or a painful misstep, the lessons you took away from the experience helped shape who you are today.

While you may feel averse to looking back for fear of exposing pain you'd rather ignore, avoiding this scrutiny precludes you from uncovering constructive insights and layers of information that can be supportive to you now.

It's possible your past choices didn't serve you or others, and it's possible that the way you made those choices leaves you scared to make future ones. Even if they weren't in your best interest, what would it take for you to forgive yourself for having made them? Imagine what could shift when you begin to view your choices as lessons and opportunities for learning.

- How might you use your wisdom to operate differently, acting with intention instead of falling into automatic patterns of behavior?

- What if you could release the pain of any choice so its aftereffects no longer anchor you to the past?

- What real lessons can be extracted from exploring a past choice?

- What were the repercussions of those choices, not just for you as an individual but for others who were touched by them?

Treasures are hidden in your past that can be used to better navigate your future.

To unearth these valuable treasures requires a willingness to look at your choices through a less judgmental lens and explore the fears, hurts and subconscious beliefs which protectively put blinders on this part of your awareness.

Contemplating and examining the details of your past with a desire to candidly acknowledge messy consequences lets you begin making peace with any shame and disappointment you've endured as a result of a perceived bad decision. Looking at your past from a mature perspective allows you to let go of pain, anger, sadness or embarrassment that you're feeling for choices you've deemed bad, that others have judged as bad or that truly resulted in bad consequences.

A year into my mapping journey, I invited a handful of women who'd explored a past choice with me to gather as a group, share what they gained from the process, and describe their insights and lessons. I sought to more fully comprehend the benefits of reckoning with past choices through their words and experiences. Meeting together online, each woman introduced herself to the others with a high-level overview of the choice she explored, why it had meaning to her and any revelations she experienced during the process. I then facilitated a conversation of collective brainstorming.

Some retold a story or shifted a limiting belief that was holding them back, some let go of guilt, some had a deeply meaningful conversation that felt different than therapy. Each expressed that after our deep-dive exploration she was able to regard her choice in a way that was less laden with judgment and disdain. All of the women recognized the value in looking back with a kind and curious mind, wondering:

- What is there for me to learn?
- Where must I heal?
- How can I use what I've gone through to evolve?

In this chapter, I'll introduce you to three of the women and will share details of their insights to clarify how addressing your past has healing potential.

Colleen, an entrepreneurial business owner from the Pacific Northwest, saw how shedding pieces of her past allowed her to step more confidently into her present. While dealing with the heaviness of her mom's dementia shortly after her dad's death, she felt burdened by the massive, dark-colored oak furniture she'd inherited which dominated the space in her adult home. For many years she lived with great anxiety that relinquishing her parents' belongings would dishonor their memory. Finally, heeding her gut's insistent nudge, and without requesting her family's permission or seeking their approval, she chose to redecorate her living room and discard her parents' dark furniture to create a light and airy space of her own. She threw away what she knew she should, invested in new items she trusted would bring her joy and incurred debt she was prepared to handle. She couldn't live their life any longer. "My kids have to grow up in our home, not my parents'," she staunchly declared.

Creating an airy room with light gray walls, a sexy white leather sofa, shag rug and a chrome and glass desk symbolized Colleen's break from outdated, stale rules. Instead of being restricted by archaic constructs, these objects became a metaphor for how she would live her life now.

Her renewed mojo at home mirrored how she began showing up differently in her business, refusing to tolerate nonsense and taking back control. Like her living room, she disposed of heavy clutter in her business.

Rather than viewing her choice to purge as a source of guilt, which she had felt for years, she understood that ridding her space of her parents' heavy, dark furniture symbolized a move forward into the present and ultimately her future.

Next, Maureen, a hard-working mom of three teenage girls, explained that she was burned out after doing so much for others—caring for her daughters, designing products for her store and putting energy into non-profit projects. In all her doing, she'd neglected to care for herself. Having always been a caregiver, she made the difficult but necessary choice to stop doing for others and focus all her energy on her well-being.

After making this choice, Maureen experienced a dramatic shift as she committed to embark on a journey to heal her younger self. Each of her girls was dealing with eating issues and it was imperative that she address the wounds around her own nutrition habits. She'd had an eating disorder for most of her youth, and while she addressed the symptoms in her twenties, she never went deep enough to unveil her more painful issues. She resented her mother for taking no action, leaving her cries unanswered.

"When it came to my daughters," she admitted, "I chose to behave differently—I became their advocate, went through their agony, dealt with their intense emotions and looked objectively at myself. Doing what I did for them, which was never done for me, provided me with an opportunity to begin healing my core wounds."

Maureen expressed that it felt deeply therapeutic to verbalize truths she'd never voiced. Most specifically, she confided to the group, she uncovered her biggest fear that the pattern of her unlearned lessons would re-emerge in her daughters.

By looking squarely at her fear without judging her mother's actions or her own, Maureen felt a renewed sense of serenity, trusting that the time she was taking for her own self-exploration and self-care was critical to best mothering herself and her daughters.

For Maureen, exploring her choice with candor gave her the validation that a choice which could easily be deemed selfish was in fact the most supportive action she could take for her well-being and that of her children.

As we moved onto Laurie, a new friend who felt like a sister, she expressed that she'd chosen to walk away from medical school and pursue naturopathic medicine—a choice she questioned incessantly. "I tend to have a hamster-wheel brain where I keep thinking the same thing over and over," she revealed.

On the surface, being a naturopath served her desire to heal the body in the gentlest way possible, but her self-imposed pressure to understand every detail of every disease was oppressive. Sitting with many unresolved questions caused Laurie deep pain and ambivalence, leaving her incapable of moving forward in her professional life.

As we discussed the nuances of Laurie's choice, she admitted that her personal roadblocks were an excuse to procrastinate and not take action—staying in limbo protected her from failing. Her way out, she discovered, was to make peace with uncertainty, not to find an answer. With a fresh perspective of seeing her past choice mapped out visually, she began to experience her future's blank space with less apprehension. With intentionality, she chose to embrace and relish the unknown and stop stressing about where she was headed.

There are times when a map is not designed to reveal something you don't know, but to allow you to make peace with a scenario you know too well.

As each woman put into words what she gained from creating her map and exploring a past choice, the common thread was a shift in perspective that allowed her to view her choice with an eye to lessons, connections and possibility instead of judgment. Their collective words about why it's beneficial to explore past choices read like guiding principles to reframe your viewpoint and see your choices as valuable lessons:

- Exploring a past choice allows you to recognize and honor your past relationships and the influence those people had in your life.

- Owning your past stories, which may be holding you back, frees you to rewrite them so they can be more supportive and constructive to who you are in the present.

- Fully acknowledging your past choices allows you to learn from them and no longer feel burdened by their weight.

- Looking back at where you've been provides you with a new vantage point to explore the possibilities of what's next for you on your journey.

- Making connections, possibly previously unnoticed, enables you to forgive, appreciate and accept both yourself and others.

Imagine these truthful statements beautifully designed on decorative cards, nugget-like, for you to contemplate and act as your guiding beacon for a moment in time. Consider that no choice you made was ever wrong—and each choice, no matter whether you view it as good or bad, was an important stepping stone laying the path to where you are today.

Real treasures are hidden in the exploration of your past, and each truth you unearth is a filter through which you can reflect on your own choices.

When you're used to repeating the same monotonous story, it can be difficult to imagine that there are other ways to interpret the facts and details, or that important truths may be obscured in your telling. As you embark on a journey to view your past choices, experiment using the reframing statements above to view your past with greater empathy. Notice which words beckon to you, and intentionally play with a new jumping off point for reflecting upon your past. Let your eyes be alert to wisdom, noticing where gold exists in even the most distressing of your experiences.

Having established the many benefits of looking back, let's examine some specific examples of past decisions.

CHAPTER 14

Past Maps in Action

As you begin the inquiry process to take stock of how a particular choice played out over time, you may detect clear gems of wisdom that were previously obscured. As a reminder, the five core Exploration Map questions to reflect upon a past choice are:

1. Why did you make this choice?
2. What fears did you have to conquer to step into this choice?
3. How did you feel when you made this choice?
4. What did you hope would happen?
5. What did you learn about yourself from this choice?

Then, to go deeper, consider these additional questions.

- How did you show up at the time?
- How did this choice impact your life?
- What people, opportunities and experiences appeared because of the momentum of your choice?
- What did you learn from this choice which changes how you approach the future?

These questions and their corresponding answers will form the foundation for your **past choice Exploration Map**. Digging into the details of your prior choices supports you to understand yourself at an earlier juncture, and to incorporate the knowledge you uncover into the arsenal of your present-day decision-making.

As we continue, I'll share the creation stories of three past Exploration Maps to demonstrate how to use questioning to make sense of a past choice. One story is my own, the other two were shared by clients.

Past Choice 1

While mapping often focuses on affirmative choices, there's great value to using this inquiry process to explore a choice you made NOT to do something—like not taking a job, not moving across the country, not getting married or not writing your book. What motivated you to initially say yes to that opportunity, and then what led you to pull back?

Just as the choices we *do* make affect our lives, so do the choices we *don't*.

Years ago, my client Evana considered moving to Hawaii to live in a missionary community with her parents. Her Exploration Map began with: *I chose not to move to Hawaii.* I took her through a set of questions similar to what I've shared with you as we unearthed the details of her choice to say no to that opportunity.

Before we examined her choice to say no to the move, I asked her to reflect on why she'd originally thought that moving was the right decision.

Answers poured out of her.

"Moving was an opportunity to live in Hawaii while my parents were establishing a Spanish-speaking congregation. The move would have allowed me to reach out to my ministry while improving my Spanish so I could connect with my family in Spain."

"What prompted you to ultimately say no?" I asked with curiosity.

"I needed a break from my dad. I wanted to create my own life and not follow my parents. My dad always tried to manage me and it was time to take control of where my life was heading," she admitted.

Evana had learned to adjust her behavior to accommodate her dad's moods, and to avoid upsetting him she never acted out. Becoming decisive strengthened her backbone to resist his domineering behavior and boldly stand up to him. The answers Evana uncovered while creating her Exploration Map enabled her to acknowledge that saying no to this move meant she was breaking from her father's firm grip. This choice established her husband as her primary relationship and positioned them to function and make decisions as a couple. During the mapping process, Evana realized that saying *no* wasn't about being afraid, but about moving forward in a way that was in her best interest.

In saying *no* to her dad, she was saying *yes* to herself.

Demonstrating the depth she chose to go with her inquiry, Evana's map became quite expansive. One leg explored why she first considered moving, while another explored what caused her to change her mind. The balance focused on details she'd never considered before, allowing her to see her decision from a more comprehensive perspective.

Using this question-and-answer practice, you can uncover the wealth of information embedded in your choices. Should you find yourself feeling self-judgment about how or why you did what you did, experiment with shifting your perspective and ask yourself:

- Based on the lessons you ultimately learned, how was your choice beneficial?

- How might you support a close friend if they were navigating a similar choice? (This question is valuable as we often speak more kindly to our friends than we do to ourselves.)

- In what ways did this choice impact you and others?

- If you were older and wiser, what might you have done differently?

As you consciously refrain from berating yourself for your past actions, engage in truth-seeking questions to expose fresh answers, eager to see what reveals itself. Accepting the lessons learned from your past choices gives you the confidence to trust yourself as you venture into making present and future choices.

Past Choice 2

A profound gift of these explorational conversations has been witnessing what becomes possible when we show interest in our deeper selves and have the humanity to view our choices and actions with compassion, benevolence and less judgment. In the following examples, I share what's possible when you explore your past with empathy.

We are each an amalgam of darkness and light and it takes great courage to expose our darkness and own what we've kept hidden. Healing comes as we embrace all parts of ourselves, seeing the pieces we may not like and choosing to accept them nonetheless. What we conceal owns us, so by not shying away from what lurks in any of our dingy, cobweb-filled corners we can acknowledge what is true, however unsavory it may be, and view it with compassion. Instead of running from what isn't pretty, allow yourself to remain curious, open to the message that's eager to reveal itself, trusting that whatever darkness is uncovered, you have the tools to cope, recover and emerge from it.

In one of my first healing maps, I explored how I'd lost myself in a past relationship and how I ultimately found my way back to a place of strength. During my journey to becoming the woman I wanted to be, I hired a coach to help me deal with my deeper emotional issues. Specifically, I wanted to heal the deep-seated wound around my self-worth that had affected how I showed up in many areas of my life since my youth. After years of repeatedly telling my unsupportive stories, I was ready to move on and shine without baggage.

As I reflected on the ending of my romantic relationship, I exposed a truth I'd been reluctant to acknowledge—I'd been showing up as a victim, a quality I judged harshly. I felt considerable shame owning that part of myself, shame I did not want to name even in the quiet of my thoughts. In spite of my humiliation, I decided to stop hiding from what I found disdainful, took ownership of my actions and looked at them with honesty and empathy. I put words to my blameworthy behavior, shared them with my trusted friends and made the commitment to shift my perspective.

Instead of looking at my life from a victim's angle asking, "what happened *to* me?" I'd ask myself: "Why is this happening *for* me? What can I learn? How can I grow?"

Past Choice 3

My client, Kathe, felt rudderless and stuck as she stepped into her mid-thirties without clear knowledge of where she was headed. With big decisions looming, she dreaded making a misstep by repeating past patterns. Not wanting to approach her present choices from a place of fear, she chose to take stock of key decisions made during the prior decade to assess what she'd learned and what had blossomed.

At first, she felt resistant to reflecting upon her past from a place of rumination and regret, worrying her finger-wagging critic would scold her for the many mistakes she felt she'd made and that feelings of regret would engulf her. To release her fear about picking the "wrong" direction, she connected to her wiser self, faithful that reflecting on her past years with grace and tenderness would invite inspiration on how to move forward.

To begin her Exploration Map, Kathe stated: *I choose to look back at the last decade with kindness.*

During her twenties, she made four key choices which ranged from choosing a new vocation, to choosing her first job, to choosing to move back in with her mother, to ultimately choosing to move out and begin dating again. For each, I asked her the following questions:

- What fundamental issues did you face as you made this choice?
- As you sat at the crossroads of this choice, what path did you not take and why?
- How did you make this choice? Was it deliberate or impulsive? Did you act on your own or have support?
- What fears did you sit with as you contemplated this choice?
- Did you have any limiting beliefs that could have held you back?
- What did you dream was possible as you stepped into this choice?
- What did making this choice demonstrate about who you are?
- What quality do you love about yourself that you can trace back to that choice?

As she processed her answers, and reflected upon the details of each choice with curiosity, I filled in the branches of her expanding Exploration Map. Each branch represented one main choice. Probing each choice in greater depth than she'd ever done before, Kathe acquired a renewed understanding of how her younger self felt at each decision's crossroad. For a few, she felt inspired, independent, open-hearted and empowered. For others she felt depleted, alone and scattered.

Resolved not to chastise herself for any choice made from a less-than-ideal mindset, Kathe set an intention that for future choices she'd check in with herself. If she was resistant, she'd dig further to uncover why. If she was feeling drained, she'd pause to focus on caring for herself so she could make her meaningful choice from a place of greater reserves. If she believed her upcoming choice was a whole-hearted yes, she'd take a deep breath to ensure she was grounded and not acting impulsively.

Having the willingness to look back over key choices made in a specific window of time is a gift you give yourself that allows you to visually see the trajectory of the paths you've taken. When you're in a dark place, it's easy to lose your bearings and feel like you're floundering with no sense of where you are, let alone where you're headed. Creating a map can expose your vulnerable spots in a way that fosters tenderness and connection instead of judgment.

As you find your orientation and understand with greater clarity how you got where you are, you can use these newly found insights to make more intentional choices as you move forward.

For your easy reference as you create a past choice Exploration Map, I've amassed a healthy list of questions related to what you hoped for, how you made your choice, what its impact was and what you learned. To access the questions, visit, http://kimdeyoung.com/ChoiceResources

CHAPTER 15

Retelling Your Story

It's not unusual when you reflect upon a past choice to create an internal story about who you were because of that choice. We then carry those stories around with us as if they're the only truth, repeating them both to ourselves and others. We often become robotic in our repetition of these stories, not even realizing we're in story-telling versus truth-telling mode.

What if the story you so cleverly concocted isn't true anymore and doesn't serve who you are at this time? Maybe you've created a story about money, or how you parent or were parented, how you showed up in a personal or professional relationship, or how you treated yourself. How does it support you to keep telling the story you're telling? How does the story serve to keep you small?

In exploring my past choices and taking others on journeys to explore theirs, I've had a unique vantage point for witnessing how tight a grip our stories have over us and how they preclude us in our quest to make healthy present-day choices. If you're anything like me, you've made choices you're not proud of. You've done something you wish you hadn't, said something you wish you didn't, hurt someone who didn't deserve it. You may be sitting with pain around the shame of a bad choice.

For your own growth and healing, it's important to let that pain go. But the question is, *how* do you let it go?

The simplest truth I've learned is: before you can let it go, you must acknowledge what you're in pain about so you can address it head on. Healing begins with awareness, and with awareness you can look at your pain for what it is, own it, and see how and where that pain is showing up so you can do the necessary work to rebuild. The I Ching reveals an elegant solution to grappling with these kinds of choices: "It's only when we have the courage to face things exactly as they are without any self-deception or illusion, that a light will develop out of events by which the path to success may be recognized."

The common theme in the exploration of past choices is that there's a story you created because of something that previously happened— how you showed up, how you were treated, how you took action (or didn't) and how you felt about yourself as a result. A story is typically born from subjective beliefs that your mind affirms as truth. Often, they're not true at all, yet because of your strong belief you create a story to validate why you think and feel what you do.

After turning fifty and re-entering the dating world, I was conscious of which stories I shared, which felt truthful to where I was in the moment, and which were outdated. I didn't want to perpetuate my old stories and bring antiquated thinking from my past into my future. I wanted the stories I told to be reflective of the work I'd done on myself. Periodically I caught myself sharing a story or a fear on auto-pilot, and as the words left my mouth, I thought, "That's old, that's not me anymore."

How many times did I catch myself regurgitating the story of being an island who could live without needing anyone? Or the one that I wasn't capable of making the money I deserve? Or the one about being emotionally neglected? As I enunciate the words, even in the writing of this book, my stomach turns.

While my words still possess some truth, with intentional cognizance I listen for the well-worn story so I can shift my language and thoughts. In the past, I recounted these stories automatically, without consciousness, letting them control my life. Now, I accept that these stories don't embody who I want to be and prompt myself to express another truth.

Just as you may zone out when driving a long distance and have no recollection of your trip from point A to B, when you're telling an old story it can pour out of you automatically. You can feel yourself going through the motions unconsciously, perhaps even anticipating the rhythm of laughter or gasps the story elicits. This is a sign you've been telling your well-crafted story for so long you're not even aware of what you're saying. The momentum of your words is bypassing the consciousness of your mind. When it feels like you're monotonously repeating a story that's past its prime, it's time to retell that story with a fresh and new perspective.

Before sharing a story, pause and consciously ask yourself, is this a truth that's relevant to the present or is it rooted in the past? When you tell a story, notice how you feel. Are you speaking your words robotically? Is there really truth in your words?

During my journey investigating people's choices, I've observed quintessential subjects that weave themselves into many stories—how you've interacted with your parents, your romantic relationships and the role that money has played in your life. These universal experiences are inextricably tied to your sense of worth, and the choices within these segments of your life frequently contain deep wells of pain and shame.

Although these experiences happened in your past, you have the opportunity today, in present time, to examine the stories you've been artfully telling on autopilot and ask yourself whether they can be recounted more honestly based on who you are today.

CHAPTER 16

Parental Relationship Stories

The next three chapters are devoted to showing you how to use map questions to retell specific types of stories—those concerning your parents, relationships and money. I've honed specific questions that will allow you to reach the deep underbelly of your story where wisdom and truth lie. Using an Exploration Map will support you to disentangle the threads so you can determine which ones are no longer integral in your future narration.

So that you can appreciate how to look at this for yourself, I'll share examples of how I've used questions in dialogue with my clients to retell more authentic and helpful stories, beginning with parental relationship stories. I purposefully didn't include map visuals in this chapter as the stories shared were guided by questions versus the map itself.

Unhealthy dynamics and unresolved tensions with our parents are ubiquitous to the point that they've become a therapy cliché—many of us can rattle off a litany of parental slights and traumas. Perhaps you've uttered the common resolution to never become like your parents, yet you've been accused of possessing the exact traits you detest in them. This foundational relationship inevitably leaves an imprint. Even if you have a secure, loving relationship with your parents, understanding your childhood experience is essential to grappling with who you've become and how you perceive the world. Might you be held back by stories you created because of labels assigned to you? Did your parents view you as the smart kid, the wild child, the screw-up, the fat girl? Are you holding onto pain from how you were raised?

Imagine what could shift if you looked back with compassion at your relationship with your parents and how they treated you. What if their parenting allowed you to learn something about yourself that's come to serve you well? What if there's an insight for you in the pain you may have suffered?

Looking at how you were parented in this way does not excuse harmful behavior, particularly abuse—this is the terrain of the trauma therapist. What we're focusing on is the process of returning to a place of empowerment when it comes to difficult parental relationships. How can we thoughtfully examine the narratives we tell ourselves about what their treatment means about us? We'll use an Exploration Map to do this.

To reflect upon your relationship with your parents, consider these questions:

- What wounds do you have from your childhood that you're ready to heal?

- What pain are you ready to release?

- What conversations must you have so you can move forward?

- What strengths did you develop because you were raised by your parents?

- What qualities about yourself do you really love that you can attribute to your parents?

- What are the positive aspects that stem from your pain?

The Exploration Map is versatile for the purposes of examining your stories. Use the questions above on your main branches and let your responses surface. I've provided an example of what this map layout looks like in the diagram on the following page.

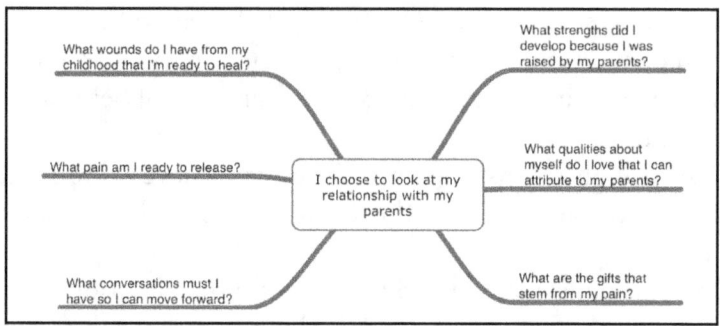

In the two stories that follow, map questions served as a springboard for reflection, each of which evolved into a deep discussion. The key takeaway to note is how powerful the process is when you seek to retell old stories through an in-depth and thoughtful question-and-answer dialogue.

Parental Relationship Story 1

Debra had been a businesswoman since opening her first lemonade stand at the age of seven. Her mom had high expectations and told her there was nothing she couldn't accomplish. She opened a checking account for Debra at age twelve and taught her budgets and spreadsheets.

Through her teen years Debra saved diligently for a down payment, and with her mother's support, qualified for a mortgage to buy her first condo at twenty-three. When she sold her first place and bought her second, she set the intention to become a real estate investor. Years later, as she and her mother adventurously drove around shopping for Debra's next real estate acquisition, her mother began making navigational mistakes. They soon discovered her mother had a brain tumor. When she died three years later, Debra imploded, screaming, "This can't be happening. She's been my guide. How will I live without her?"

Debra vacillated between wanting to live up to her mother's expectations and wanting to find her own way. "My mother always pushed me because she believed in my competence, but I've often wondered who I'd be if I didn't have to be successful."

"How have you reconciled her expectations of you?" I inquired.

"Her beliefs guided me when she was alive, but after her death my life went in a different direction and her messages stopped resonating with me," she said. "It's been challenging to move on without all the pressure of who she wanted me to be. She believed I'd be a mogul, her definition of success, but that was her expectation of me, not mine."

"What would it feel like to let go of the pressure of being a mogul?" I questioned.

"That's tough to answer. I was raised to believe I should always be self-reliant, and never be the woman who allows herself to be provided for."

"Do those beliefs feel true to you at this time?" I curiously asked.

"I don't think they do," she said, looking inward for the answer. "If I look at them with fresh eyes, they don't work for me any longer. I've never really cared about being a mogul, and it'd feel great if that wasn't who I had to be. I'd love to live a life where being successful was not how I defined myself."

"What if that's the new choice you make today?" I proposed. "What new truth would you like to step into?"

"It's not that I won't be financially successful, it's just not my primary goal. I want to lead with my heart, and then my leadership will follow."

Arriving at that realization, Debra had an opportunity, in the privacy of her inner conversations, to reconsider how she spoke of herself. Freeing herself from the outdated story that she hadn't met her mother's expectations, she reframed her thoughts so she could move onto a path that was more personally meaningful and rewarding.

Parental Relationship Story 2

Like Debra's mom, my father always had high expectations of me. I was the "boy" of the family who he believed could accomplish anything, and I was valued for my competence and independence. The challenge of his high expectations was that he perpetually wanted more: "You got an A, where's the A+?" This omnipresent, never-achieving-enough question drove me to continually strive for the A+, incapable of accepting myself as the A, always feeling whatever I did was not good enough.

While my wiser self grasped the benevolent paternal motivation of his seemingly innocuous question, it didn't ease my pain of feeling inadequate. My belief of not being enough percolated beneath the surface of my psyche for years, at the heart of many therapy sessions, hindering me from shining as brightly as I dreamt.

As I progressed in my early career, I made two professional choices that my father found incomprehensible, causing him to question my decision-making ability. The first was my choice to walk away from an established company for an unknown start-up. The second involved leaving the start-up to move across the country to San Francisco to work for the Gap.

For both, I had an extraordinary opportunity to learn new skills and work with smart people, while getting to travel and work in an environment that was creative and exciting.

For both, he asked apprehensively, "What if it doesn't work? What will you do?"

For both, I responded with the bravado of a woman in her early twenties: "I'll be fine—I'll still have the foundation of me and all I've learned, and I'll get another job."

How could he not get it? I wondered. *I'd be traveling overseas frequently, working for great companies and continually increasing my salary.*

For me, each choice was a no-brainer. For him, they triggered uncertainty about my boldness and willingness to take sudden leaps.

As I rose quickly through the ranks, I sat in a place of conflict. While I knew I was good at what I did, I incessantly questioned why I was paid so much. I nursed deep doubts about my value, and as my salary continued to escalate the disparity between my worth and my earnings grew, causing me to feel like a fraud.

It took over a decade to trace this tension back to the messages of my childhood. From my exchanges with my dad I'd internalized the attitude that I should continually strive toward the next step, settling for nothing short of excellence. For each achievement there was little fanfare, no pat on the back, just a nod and a nudge to work harder and continue my ascent. This double-edged sword motivated me, but also led me to believe that whatever I was doing, and ultimately, who I was, was not enough. In moments when I didn't feel proficient because I was starting something new or making a bold and risky choice, I lost sight of my self-worth because I'd conflated it with competence and mastery.

For much of my young adulthood I pointed the finger at my father, blaming him for relentlessly pushing me with what felt like unrealistic expectations. I created the narrative that no matter how well I did, how smart I was or how much money I made, it wasn't good enough for him.

Looking at my story from a parental perspective of my dad's thinking and intentions, I now understand he never sought to make me feel inadequate. He was a father who believed in his daughter and pushed her to realize her potential. Witnessing the victim-like story I told for many years through an adult lens allowed me to begin releasing the idea that I was valued for my performance more than for who I was.

As I've grown to comprehend more about my father, I have greater sensitivity for my relationship with my children and for the impact that my words, actions and expectations have upon them. And yet I accept that it will be part of their path of learning and growth to unravel their own narratives and potentially retell the stories they're so artfully creating based on their own experiences and perceptions.

Thoughtfully interrogating your relationship with your parents exposes the many ways that childhood experiences shape what comes next, and also puts you in the position to take charge of what persists further.

CHAPTER 17

Romantic Relationship Stories

Being in a romantic relationship is a gift for your personal growth and development. Your partner acts as a mirror for all you're experiencing and how you're growing, reflecting back your light and your darkness. Whether they were the best or worst partner, how you interacted with them provides you with an opportunity to take responsibility for your behavior so you can look at your actions honestly, release any unwanted baggage and enter future relationships with greater clarity and consciousness.

Being fully present and doing the work of deeply exploring the uncharted aspects of a relationship exposes hidden parts of yourself. Looking back at past romantic relationships allows you to reflect upon why you stayed, how you showed up, how the relationship benefitted you, what you learned, and what it took, or will take, to completely let them go.

Looking back on your romantic relationships, consider these questions:

- Why did you stay in the relationship?
- In what ways was this relationship similar or different to the primary romantic relationships you witnessed as a child?
- In what ways did this relationship benefit you? Or hurt you?
- How did you show up?
- What do you need to forgive in yourself or your partner?

- What did you learn that you will do, or not do, in a future relationship? (The information you capture in this answer is important to hold onto as you embark on your next relationship.)
- What will it take for you to fully let that relationship go?

To map these questions about your relationship stories, use the template below as a springboard.

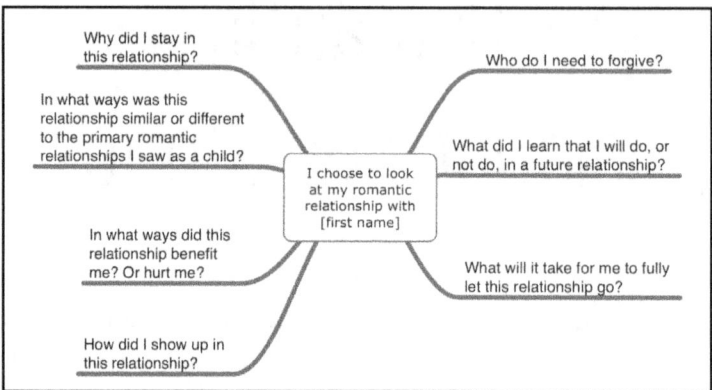

Romantic Relationship Story 1

You've likely created stories about yourself based on how your relationships have gone—a way to explain why things went the way they did. These are narratives like, *she left me, so I must be unlovable*, or, *I can't trust myself to choose a worthy partner*. Left unexamined, relationship stories can then become self-fulfilling. Rather than acting how you'd like to act, you act in accordance with what you believe about yourself, and then it seems as if the events of your life confirm this negative story. It's not until you break the cycle of the story that you can shift the narrative.

Beth, a woman I'd grown up with, wanted to explore and heal the shame she felt because she chose to stay in an abusive relationship. Before marrying Michael, she knew he became angry and volatile when he drank, but as a twenty-year-old with a chip on her shoulder because she didn't have a college degree, she didn't have the confidence to leave. She feared living on her own and catastrophized that he'd take everything, including the kids. She perpetuated a demoralizing story with herself in the role of the victim.

As their three boys grew, Michael continued to be emotionally abusive. Beth was submissive and afraid of his temper—she taught her sons to say the right thing, be polite and scatter when their dad was angry. She felt excruciating shame that she hadn't taken greater control to prevent her children from succumbing to their dad's alcoholic abuse.

When her boys became teens, after years of being bullied, Beth chose to take a stand for herself. She befriended a group of women who championed her, connecting her to inner strength she'd never before tapped into. She acknowledged she didn't need to stay in her marriage and realized that leaving Michael was a viable option. She grew more independent, stopped fearing he'd walk away leaving her with nothing, and trusted she had the wherewithal to handle whatever circumstances arose.

"How did your new perspective allow you to shift as a mother?" I questioned.

"As the boys got older and I did a lot of personal growth work, I accepted that I can't fix what's already happened. I spoke candidly with each of them and stated very directly, 'You need to move on and make your own choices.'"

As she shared the details of her initial choice to stay in the abusive relationship, and then her subsequent choice to take a stand for herself, it became apparent that her victim story was obsolete. She was ready to release her old persona and tell a new story that reflected her growth, healing and renewed strength.

Romantic Relationship Story 2

At thirty-nine, my client Stephanie, a high-powered corporate attorney, anticipated that the next man who crossed her path would likely be "the one". She and Andrew had similar connections, she trusted him and he was pleasant to be around. As an added benefit, her mother loved that his Ivy League MBA trumped Stephanie's education. With the superficial boxes checked, she chose to marry him.

In the background, there were many niggling red flags. She wondered why he'd stayed married to his ex-wife as long as he had when she abused drugs. She dismissed her inner nudges to look more deeply into his money issues when it was apparent his financial management skills were awful; he never kept any of his windfalls and he was deeply in debt. Wanting to enter their marriage with a clean slate, she chose to pay off his debts without having the difficult and necessary money conversation. She'd let the external approval of his higher education cloud her judgment.

Over the years, Stephanie gradually recognized the truth of Andrew's character and acknowledged the cracks in the foundation of their marriage. In spite of her concerns, she opted to stay married because she enjoyed the marital perks and wished to avoid the mess of a divorce. When she looked more honestly at why she stayed, she acknowledged that codependency was the root of her issue. Her pattern of controlling every situation and feeling a responsibility to rescue others was one she recognized from her past.

Equipped with greater awareness, Stephanie chose to dissolve her marriage and leave with grace. She chose to show up with greater courage in her divorce than she had in her marriage, allowing herself to feel powerful during her process of leaving. In focusing on rebuilding her economic security, she studied how to get divorced, separate their assets, protect herself and plan her exit.

From this stance of greater empowerment, she owned that she'd neglected her inner voice and resolved not to disregard her internal compass moving forward. Wanting to be a role model for her nieces and demonstrate that they have the ability to stand on their own, she chose to stop letting things happen to her and took responsibility for what was occurring in her life. No longer would she tell the story of blindly following a man with a fancy pedigree, but instead, she'd create a new story in which she was the protagonist.

Romantic Relationship Story 3

We've each had a meaningful relationship end that's left us assessing how to best rebuild ourselves. Whether or not you were the one to end it, investing the time and energy to heal is paramount to keeping your past baggage out of future relationships.

After her divorce, my client Lara, a single mom to two boys, threw herself wholeheartedly into a long-distance, multi-year relationship that ended in heartbreak. Once she came out of her darkness and regained her composure, she was eager to address her role in their break-up so she wouldn't perpetuate her behavior when she stepped into something new.

She'd given herself to this relationship more completely than any other. It was both a gift and a source of pain that her partner mirrored back her greatest strengths as well as her greatest weaknesses. He shared that she'd lost herself, and at times had shown up as a victim. He felt they'd become too much of a "we" and lost the individuality of their identities. Lara elected not to shrink from the harshness of his words and trusted that by facing his observations head on, there was gold for her growth on the other side.

She acknowledged the embarrassing truth that she loved him more than she loved herself, which was not sustainable in any relationship. While it caused her great shame to ask how and why she found herself in this position, she chose not to hide from exploring the answers that lay beneath.

"Initially, I felt victimized, since he broke up with me," she confided, "but sitting in the victim's role only fostered me wallowing in my pain versus moving through it."

Exploring deep layers of her truth via an Exploration Map allowed Lara to shift her perspective and ask more thought-provoking questions.

- Why might their breakup be happening for her?
- What could she learn from this experience?
- Where is there an opportunity for her growth?
- What is this situation teaching her about herself?

Ready to move on, she chose to find her way back to herself—the self-possessed woman she knew lingered within. As a people-pleaser, she'd invested more energy in giving to others and lost touch with what it meant to love herself. She chose to embark on a solo journey where she demonstrated a willingness to be alone so she could find new ways to connect with herself, and develop an enthusiasm for her life that was independent of a man.

Choosing to be alone allowed her to focus on doing what made her happy, saying yes as often as possible, and saying no to anything that felt intuitively off. She consciously treated herself the way she wanted to be treated and saw that her happiness and strength were the source of her self-worth, not a relationship. She focused on cultivating trust that she'd meet the right man rather than forcefully making it happen.

She chose to open herself to other relationships only when she felt she was in good company with herself.

When a relationship ends, it's critical to reflect on why and take responsibility for your part in it. Romantic relationships, especially when you've shown up with openness and vulnerability, are the most wonderful mirror of your less-than-perfect spots. Once you observe and acknowledge these tender areas, you can determine with consciousness how you want to show up next.

- What pieces of your story will you continue to tell?
- What pieces are best left in the past?
- What can you acknowledge and own about yourself so you don't repeat past unhealthy patterns?

CHAPTER 18

Money Relationship Stories

Like our romantic partners, we're also in a relationship with money—good or bad, healthy or problematic. We carry beliefs and values passed down from past generations—what our parents and their parents were taught to believe about money, how they earned their living and how they imparted their values to us. We bring our money legacy with us into our relationships as we internalize our family's stories and set forth into the world to either follow their path or not. Each is a choice.

Your personal money stories are a combination of how you've internalized your family's money beliefs coupled with your own experiences making, spending and saving money. You then have the choice about whether you perpetuate these stories. How do you let go of messages you deem unhealthy, and shift your language and belief system to one that is more aligned with your present values?

Your relationship with money is an opportunity for you to examine issues of self-worth and shame, among other things. Here are some questions that can act as a helpful doorway:

- What does money mean to you?
- What was the relationship your primary caregivers had with money and what does that tell you about your relationship with money?
- What limiting beliefs do you have about money?
- What narratives do you have about people who have a lot of money?

- What narratives do you have about people who have less?

- What story have you created about yourself around money?

As you reflect upon these questions, you can begin the process of releasing any unsupportive legacy stories you've perpetuated, and bring consciousness to how you'll reframe the stories you tell about money's role in your life. Using the map template below will provide you with a good starting point for reflection.

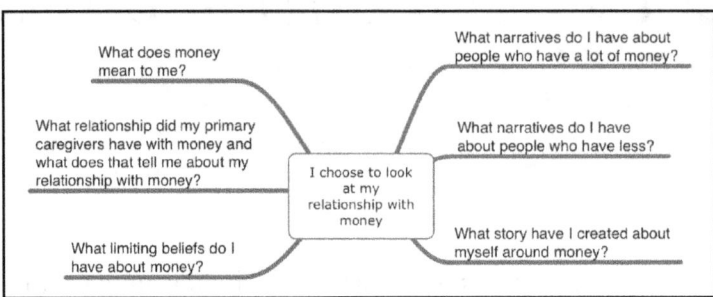

Money Relationship Story 1

Stories are often born from small moments which have the power to entwine themselves around the core of your being, affecting how you see and view yourself.

My client Sally was raised in a home where no one spoke of money and the silence around this taboo topic felt deafening. As a twenty-something finding her way and earning her own income, she felt bad for cautiously declining friends' proposals for fun opportunities because they felt outside her financial reach. Her parents shielded her from money conversations because their own childhood experiences were devoid of these discussions. They didn't speak candidly of their financial issues or anxieties, leaving Sally to feel isolated and without a roadmap for how to handle the new concerns and questions surfacing for her as a young adult.

Whether your parents had a lot or a little affects how they behaved with money and the messages they shared. You then formulated your own values and money stories based on what you perceived. You may feel guilty if you're not in financial alignment with your family, making more, spending more or saving less. Your relationship with money may be highly charged as it's directly related to your self-worth and is often a barometer for your definition of success.

Money Relationship Story 2

To uncover the truth of my money story, I've ventured into my darkest corners, using both maps and therapy to expose my legacy money beliefs so that I could begin the reframing and healing process.

From an early age I grasped the tension between my parents as I witnessed them sitting on opposite sides of the financial spectrum. Not wanting to get caught in their separate values, I felt bad if I spent and bad if I asked. By acknowledging my father's beliefs, would I alienate my mother and cause a rift? If I owned her beliefs, would that separate me from my friends who were living more carefree? What about the story of how these beliefs have affected my self-worth, how I show up as a parent and how I now impart my money story to my children?

At twelve, switching from a public school in the suburbs to a private school in the city, my awareness quickly adjusted to the faster pace of my city friends as compared to my sheltered suburban life. Wanting to fit in, I asked my mother for a pair of Pro-Keds.

"No, those are too expensive and you don't need them," she quickly retorted.

Shopping at discount stores became a barrier separating me from the other kids, who most always had some version of a designer label on their pants.

Years later, coveting a beautiful and expensive pair of shoes, I asked my dad for money, a furtive request my mother couldn't know about. Covertly, he handed me two crisp one hundred dollar bills, a transaction I understood was meant to remain between us. The story I internalized was that he believed I was a good kid who wanted something a bit frivolous, he had the money, and in the big picture of my life, what did it really matter? For my mom, just asking for the shoes, let alone getting them, signified I'd gone to the dark side and would ultimately believe I was a princess entitled to whatever I wanted.

When I began to make a significant amount of money a few years later thanks to my burgeoning corporate career, it felt like more than I deserved. While I knew I was good at what I did, I didn't yet appreciate my value.

Entering my marriage in my thirties with a healthy nest egg, I used that money to put the down payment on our first house, fund the startup of my first entrepreneurial venture, and cover the shortfall during many financially tenuous years. While I didn't see my spending as flagrant, and felt pleased that I had resources to do what I wanted and needed without asking for help, a shameful and unspoken truth permeated my insomnia-induced thoughts: I was spending money like a rich girl who could, which was anathema to my mother's beliefs.

I internalized the judgment she placed on spending she regarded as flagrant, and consciously didn't share the specifics of my business spending with my husband, best friend or parents.

As the path of my married life twisted and turned and my husband went through various job losses, the pot of money we relied upon dwindled more quickly than expected as it supported my business and covered our deficit. Although I thought I was cleverly hiding our financial stress, my parents sensed what was happening and confronted me in an intervention to share their concerns.

"Pull it together," my mother emphatically stated without any sugar-coating, "you're acting irresponsibly and putting your family at risk."

When my marriage ended, I began diving deeply into my stories and unspoken truths to explore my culpability. While it was too late to repair the broken bonds of our marriage, I could change the course of my future by exposing my conditioning around money and taking steps to become more conscious of its role in my life. I made a new choice: *I choose that my past money story, and all the shame it's embodied, will no longer define who I am.* With that choice clearly stated, I committed to begin the process of retelling my legacy story to release the version I'd held since adolescence.

I developed a daily mapping practice to support myself to not backslide into the comfort of my tired, unsupportive narrative. My process involved either reflecting upon one truth already within my money map, or assessing if I'm meant to add a new one. Investing just a few moments concentrating and grounding myself in my consciously written statements supported me to maintain vigilance that I walk forward on the path of my choice.

By developing awareness of your money stories, you have the opportunity to see what's true and what's obsolete.

Regardless of whether the characters in your story recall your experience, or question if your observations are "real" or not, what you've conjured from one or many interactions has the potential to take on great importance. From our stories come our beliefs, and those beliefs then lead us to perpetuate the stories, and the cycle continues.

As you examine where your story began, consider what it will take to narrate a fresh story that's aligned with where you want to go. What thoughts and language can you shift to move yourself in a new direction? How may it have benefitted you to continue telling your story, even though each time you heard it cross your lips you knew it was outdated?

As you connect to a more authentic and supportive version of your money story, you create opportunities for money dialogues with your children. Instead of passively handing down legacy ideas about money and worth, you can nurture money consciousness as you share the educational parts of your truth, guiding them to question and examine their beliefs and stories while they make the best decisions on their path.

When you look honestly through the archives of your life, you may find that the stories you've been living and rehashing are fictitious—woven together from countless threads of tired narratives, limiting beliefs and fears. Should this be your experience, you can make the decision to unravel the details of these stories that are taking up space on the shelves of your internal library and retell them.

What will it take to release the story and reframe your perspective so you can reveal a new truth?

You can't change the past, but you can change what the past means.

CHAPTER 19

Releasing Shame and Moving to Forgiveness

"Can I see a show of hands of anyone who didn't make a mistake or do something they regretted at twenty-two?" Monica Lewinsky asked her audience in her 2015 TED Talk, *The Price of Shame.*

In making her choice to fall in love with the President of the United States, Monica transitioned from being a completely private figure to one who was publicly humiliated worldwide. After experiencing devastatingly dark days, the benevolence and empathy from her family, friends, professionals and sometimes even strangers saved her.

"Shame can't survive empathy," she stated, quoting researcher Brené Brown. "Anyone who's suffering from shame and public humiliation needs to know one thing: You can survive it. It may not be painless, quick or easy, but you can insist on a different ending to your story—have compassion for yourself."

We've all made decisions that led to shame and regret, though probably not to the level Monica experienced. Our feelings are often stowed away, and we expend great energy concealing them. Each of us has one face we show the world, and one we keep hidden. Our lives are like a house with many rooms. We proudly share those that are beautifully decorated, while keeping the dilapidated rooms hidden from view. How many people do you willingly invite into your home to see all your rooms?

It's one thing to have empathy for your darkness and view it with limited judgment. It's quite another to unabashedly expose what you've deliberately kept beneath the veil. You may assume if someone knew the details of your shame, they'd reject or leave you. If they knew your painful truths, could they love and understand you?

To move forward it's imperative that you address your shameful wounds honestly and clean them up. Being willing to step into the muck and accept what you don't like about your actions, and your thoughts, requires courage. The only way out is through.

Until you acknowledge and own the consequences of your choices, you can't choose differently.

If you had your older, wiser, more experienced self to ask for support at the time you made your less-than-perfect choice, you likely wouldn't have made it. Yet you didn't, so you did, and it's important to forgive yourself and acknowledge your humanness.

By taking an intentional and deliberate look inward you can view your choices with a sense of curiosity and tenderness, revealing how and why you made them, ideally without judgment. Once laid bare, there is less need to scrutinize the past, second-guess your actions and relive your experiences.

Shame, when shared, loses its power.

Similar to a balloon filled with air, you can strain and contort to hold your shame inside, but once it's safely shared with someone you trust, it dissipates and your tightly-held grip lessens.

There is forgiveness to be granted for what you did or thought, and more importantly, for how your actions left you feeling. Your actions are rarely as horrible as the story you've so cleverly crafted.

As you develop greater consciousness around choice, you can state what you'd like to do differently. You can articulate what may be holding you back and set the intention to proceed in a new way that reflects what you've learned. You don't want to be scared of X because you have baggage from Y. You don't want to fear entering a new relationship because of what happened with previous ones.

Recalling some of your past choices may stir up shame. You may feel shame for things you don't speak about or even acknowledge to yourself. You may feel shame for how you've treated others, how you've treated yourself or how others treated you. You may feel shame for how you've spent money, what you've chosen to eat and how you've lied to others about how you're living your life.

Sitting with shame may cause you to feel inadequate, embarrassed, not good enough or unloved. The shame you harbor often goes unspoken to anyone—your dearest friends, your closest family, even your deepest self. Sometimes shame sits in the forefront of your thoughts. Other shame resides in the deep recesses of your mind, not accessible for conscious recollection but insidiously damaging who you have the potential to be and become.

Shame can isolate you. Shame can cause you to feel no one would ever understand what you've done or what you've gone through. Shame can leave you feeling judged and alone.

Shame is rooted in past actions, past choices, past thoughts. Guilt is the emotion you feel when you've done something wrong. Shame is the emotion you feel when you believe you've been wrong.

Of the many Exploration Map conversations I've had, the most gut-wrenching was with a woman who made the choice to escape a captor who'd lured her into a cult. She harbored unconscionable amounts of shame for having stayed as long as she did, and held onto countless limiting beliefs after she left. Was she damaged goods? Was she naive for not knowing how dangerous her situation was? Was she stupid for ignoring her intuition and getting herself into the heinous situation to begin with?

Not wanting to rein her in as she shared her story, I barely spoke for two hours. Actually, I barely breathed. The gravity of her words filled our space as she recounted in three-dimensional detail the agony of a story she'd rarely spoken in its totality.

Although she ultimately made the choice to leave, she feared others wouldn't understand that she'd been mentally coerced—told she had to endure this experience for her own good. She feared a worse fate awaited her on the other side of her escape.

In the creation of her map, she focused on her commitment to excavate the details of her experience, not shying away from what was deeply uncomfortable. To move through and beyond it was imperative that she address the harsh truths of what occurred.

During our debrief several weeks after her harrowing exploration, she described how freeing it was to share so much so quickly, and in such depth. Speaking her truth was a powerful catalyst for a break-through in her healing. By dissecting the excruciating emotional layers from that experience, she could visualize her life from an aerial perspective, in its entirety, and see the reality of all that occurred.

With additional therapeutic support after her mapping experience, she released some of the negative programming and painful self-doubt she'd held from that traumatic event. She observed how looking back at her past, even though it was horrific, gave her the perspective to close the chapters she wanted to conclude. Putting the past behind her helped her refocus her energy on cultivating neglected areas of her life.

While your choices may not be as dramatic as joining and then escaping a cult, chances are you've made choices that deeply impacted your view of the world—choices that created feelings of shame, that altered important relationships, that you didn't share candidly with others.

Much of what holds us back—shame, feeling like a fraud, fear and guilt—is common to the human experience, yet we work hard to keep it hidden.

During her mapping session, Lissa, a new friend with whom I felt a deep connection, unearthed the buried shame she felt around a choice she made three decades earlier. Until our conversation, she'd not fully shared the extent of her internal anguish with anyone, including her husband.

Lissa decided to have her son at nineteen after being shamed by her mother for an abortion as a young teen. Having her son spurred a second choice—to leave college—which created a core wound of feeling inadequate compared to anyone with a diploma. Her long-ago choice launched a downward spiraling force in her life, preventing her from stepping out as she dreamt.

"I've always played small," she sheepishly confessed. "That piece of paper would have allowed me to feel better about myself."

Although she grew a successful business, she overcompensated daily, painstakingly keeping her long-held secret obscured. When Lissa voiced her misery to me about leaving college, she acknowledged it was one of the few times she'd ever spoken this truth.

So often we exert an enormous amount of energy concealing the past and burying its scars, yet there's something freeing about facing the dark parts of our lives, sharing them in a safe space and recognizing the imprint they leave. Once the truth is expressed, you can use your resources to cope and move forward. You can see more clearly how the pain you hold is affecting your life and begin to undertake the work of healing.

It's paramount to address your shame (and its nefarious sister, judgment) so their insidious claws don't erode your self-esteem and preclude you from making new and healthy choices. Rather than looking at shame as something horrible to ignore and avoid, you can shift to viewing it as a gift—an internal signal that you have healing work to do. Facing shame head-on is an opportunity to see that you have coping skills, that you're stronger than you often realize and that the stories your shame has been telling you aren't true.

When you have the courage to wade through the muck of your shame, you heal.

To release shame, the most powerful choice you can make is to forgive yourself. To release resentment, the most powerful choice you can make is to forgive others for how their choices affected you. Forgiveness is not about negating the experience of what happened, but seeing with compassion and understanding that those choices, which may not have been the healthiest, were the other person's lessons.

Harboring shame and resentment keeps you rooted in your past. Forgiveness doesn't change the past; it sets you up to change the future.

I met Richard at a workshop shortly after I began mapping and was eager to explore the choice he took to embark on a big leadership role with a prominent guru in the personal development space. While he initially feared working closely with this leader, once he said yes, he took his choice seriously and stepped wholeheartedly into the role. As a result of his significant leadership experience, he gained great visibility within the organization and was asked to run additional coaching programs.

Years later, while he was professionally soaring, Richard was publicly chastised by the head of human resources for how he'd handled an awkward circumstance with another team member. Humiliated, he was forced to resign and subsequently blamed her for the end of this dream job.

"Was there good that came from feeling so bad?" I questioned.

"There always is later on, when you can see it. Working with a therapist after months of explosive anger and bottomless despair, I chose to forgive this woman for her actions, which was a challenging but cathartic experience."

"What came from your choice to forgive her?"

"A new opportunity presented itself that I'm convinced never would have happened had I stayed in an angry, vindictive place." he explained. "I got a chance to play in a rich sandbox full of extraordinary people, affording me the ability to cultivate new relationships and step into something even bigger."

"When you think about this woman now, what comes to mind?"

"I'd always described her as the bitch who ruined my life and caused me to lose a job I loved. But, as we're speaking, I see I have an opportunity to shift my story around her."

"In what way?" I asked curiously.

"I perpetuated the story that she destroyed my life, but that's not true. It was only as a result of our experience that I was forced to look within and forgive, which I'm convinced led to new opportunities that came my way."

With conscious awareness, Richard released the resentment he felt toward this woman.

By looking at his past from a safe space, he reframed an unhealthy story. His ability to forgive enabled him to see the situation from a fresh perspective and acknowledge his growth.

Finding the compassion to forgive yourself can often be more challenging than forgiving another.

When my client Melody showed up to our coaching call after a many-month hiatus, she shared her embarrassment for not having taken action on tasks we'd spoken about months earlier.

Like Melody, you may have set out to make a change yet found yourself mired in the same place months later. While it feels like a personal failing, it's incredibly common to repeat patterns out of fear, busy-ness and inertia. In a moment of uncertainty, as you seek to do something new, the quibbling voices of doubt and past conditioning steer you toward doing what's familiar. Stepping back to view your pattern honestly removes some of the emotional charge so you can return to inquiry and intentional action. What must you do to break out of your slump, and just as importantly, not berate yourself for having been stagnant?

Each morning, when you wake feeling stuck or unhappy you can make a new choice to do what matters to you. This door of possibility is available to you every day. While it's helpful from a place of learning to own why you didn't do what you set out to do, it's not helpful to approach your assessment from a place of judgment.

What will it take to let go of shame and embarrassment and forgive yourself for what you did not do, while also setting yourself up to learn from it? Stepping into a space of courageous awareness allows you to examine why you did not take your desired actions—not from a place of self-judgment, but from a place of growth.

- What fears got in your way?
- What excuses did you create that prevented you from doing what mattered to you?
- What were you able to avoid by not taking action?
- What can you learn as you apply what you did in the past to what you may do next?

To provide you with a starting point, these questions are shown in map form.

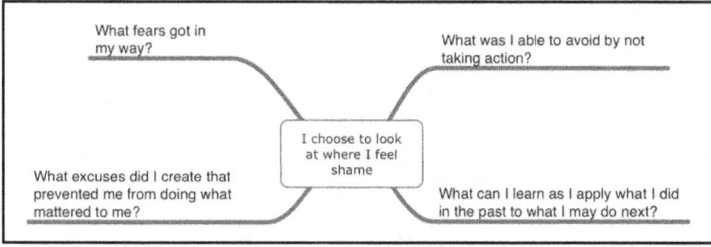

When you look at the past with these questions in mind, you learn forgiveness, appreciation and acceptance. Examining your past choices with the goal of forgiveness frees you to recognize and honor their influence in your life. Rather than continually berating yourself, which may keep you stuck in a cycle of scarcity and shame, choose to forgive yourself and use that learning to shift how you make future decisions.

As you develop a clearer understanding of how you got where you are, instead of bemoaning it or feeling like a failure, see with certainty the choices that could lead you forward. You have the power to create deliberate change in your life.

To support you in creating a past choice Exploration Map, I've compiled the questions from this chapter into a list with visual templates. You can access these resources at http://kimdeyoung.com/ChoiceResources.

PART 5

Future Choices
Finding Your Way

You do not need to know precisely what is happening,
or exactly where it is all going. What you need is to recognize
the possibilities and challenges offered by the present moment,
and to embrace them with courage, faith and hope.
−Thomas Merton

CHAPTER 20

The Possibility
of a Future Choice

A future choice is something you want, something you may not have done before, something that beckons. Looking into the blank vista of your future, you're confronted with the duality of abounding possibility and threatening uncertainty.

As you contemplate a future choice, conjuring up what's possible, it may feel both thrilling and terrifying as you question: ***How will I get to that place in the distance?***

Future choices frequently feel remote, undefined and improbable. They're habitually accompanied by apprehension as your mind becomes congested with dread of potential problems and reasons to stay put.

You may be young, just finishing school and ready to embark upon your life and career, yet feel immobilized by all that's open to you. How do you begin the journey?

Or you may have lived as an adult and realize you're unsettled and where you are isn't where you want to be. How do you find your way to that elusive place you imagine, and perhaps even long for? What does it look like to navigate your way toward what you care about?

When reflecting upon a past choice, your perspective is one of inquiry. When considering a present choice, your perspective is presence. When imagining a future choice, your perspective is one of possibility.

Your previous choices established the foundation for where you are now. Your present and future decisions set the course for where you're going.

Moving forward calls for courage and trust that you'll be able to navigate the unknown. It takes letting go of limiting beliefs that may have encumbered you in the past. It takes having faith that you can handle whatever arises.

The human brain is conditioned to focus on what doesn't work, what isn't possible and what can't be done as a way to keep us safe. We erect roadblocks that leave us feeling powerless, though we actually have far more control over our lives than we realize.

It's an adventure to take agency of your life and find your way from where you are to where you want to go. As you imagine a future choice, indulge yourself by luxuriating in what's possible, envisioning how that choice may change the trajectory of your life. Do you dream of doing something purpose-filled and soul-enhancing? Is being in a loving relationship something you crave? What about the push-pull you feel about engaging in an activity that scares you?

Connecting to possibility through questioning builds enthusiasm and motivation. It gives you a deeper sense of *why* that can bolster you through the journey. As you open yourself up with questions that inspire possibility, an Exploration Map will serve as the vehicle to delve into your answers in greater depth. Many of the questions you'll ask are similar to those you ask for present choices, but you'll approach the choosing and mapping process with a more expansive, potential-oriented mindset.

What choice can you make today that has the potential to change your life's path for the better?

This question encourages you to contemplate a future choice you may not have considered before, or that may be lurking in the background of your thoughts. While each future choice is not necessarily life-altering, reflecting on this question can help to awaken you from the monotony of daily life.

Might you choose to:

• Write a book?

• Work with a new coach?

- Take a stand for yourself?
- Let go of something that no longer serves you?
- Embark on a journey of self-care?
- Let your voice be heard?
- Heal a relationship that matters to you?
- Travel somewhere unknown?
- Tackle something you've avoided because it felt scary?
- Work with a new client whose work matters greatly to you?
- Meet an amazing partner who makes you deliriously happy?

The choice need not be big and life-defining, but it must matter to you and get you excited. It must feel fun and juicy, not heavy, cumbersome and filled with "should" energy. You're making this choice because you want to, not because you feel you must.

Imagining what's possible balances the scales that would otherwise be tipped downward by the discomfort of uncertainty. Your journey to possibility begins with movement. What choice will you make today that will set you in motion?

In the chapters that follow, I'll support you with questions to generate possibility and action as you become your own guide and find your way into the future—that place you want to go but can't quite see.

Building a Future Map

The process for building a future map is the same as the process for building past and present maps—ask a question and listen for the response. The answer becomes a branch that leads to the next question.

Uncertainty, anxiety and outdated stories often muddle the blank space of the future. Creating a future map provides you with a framework to sort your thoughts, document your stressors and organize your plans to facilitate your progression into the distance. In adding dimension to your Exploration Map through question-and-answer, you're scaffolding your future with language to navigate the unknown.

The foundational Exploration Map questions will serve as the starting point for your inquiry.

- Why does this choice matter to you?
- What fears (or limiting beliefs) might get in your way of stepping into the choice?
- How do you want to show up as you make your decision?
- What may become possible because you make this choice?
- What actions will you take to bring your choice to life?

The responses that bubble up are a rough draft. As you let your answers flow freely, know that you can return to the map to finesse your words, becoming more precise with your language until it speaks a truth that resonates.

My son's twenty-two-year-old friend craved guidance as he began navigating a future choice. Having been an avid rock climber since junior high, he was curious to explore what his life might be like without climbing. Feeling the weight of adult professional responsibilities as he transitioned into the world of medicine, he wanted to consider adjustments in how he spent his time.

"Before we begin your map, let's bring specificity to the wording of your choice," I proposed. "Which statement resonates with you more?"

- I choose to explore my life without climbing.
- Or, I choose to explore what may come into my life without climbing.

"Without a doubt, it's the second one," he said. "That one better communicates the future I'm curious to explore and the question I want to answer."

The way you frame a choice matters, and a map is a space to refine the wording of your intentions. As you continue engaging with your map, devote energy to bringing precision to your words. By fine-tuning your language, the vision for your future will blossom with continually unveiled connections, insights and possibilities.

During the initial creation of a future map, the ideas captured may feel cursory and simplistic. This is natural—your map is taking shape as you gradually tap into the essence of what you truly want. Enjoy the process of letting your choice and map evolve, adding branches and updating your words over time. There's a richness in building a future map in stages, to returning to it after it's had time to percolate, to noodling your words until they embody and truly represent what you idealize. As your map develops, trust that with continued inquiry, insightful questions will surface, allowing your map to slowly ripen with all you're discerning.

For future mapping, I recommend sitting in a ritualized manner for short periods of time—five minutes of focused attention within a map over a few days or weeks is sufficient for it to grow. Setting a time limit provides a helpful boundary to ease the pressure and expectation of getting to a specific answer immediately.

I've laid out the Exploration Map questions for a future choice, along with additional questions to take your map deeper, in their own section on the resources page at http://kimdeyoung.com/ChoiceResources.

Creating a future map brings intentionality to your choice as you acknowledge that you're initiating movement toward the future you want. Proceeding forward in the direction of what matters to you requires trusting that you can begin the journey and course-correct if necessary, making thoughtful choices at each crossroads, finding your way incrementally.

Now that we've discussed the future mapping process, let's return to the guiding idea of this section: ***How will you get to that place in the distance?***

You'll get there by using the Exploration Map questions as your guide—specifically, fleshing out your answers to the last two Exploration Map questions that are rich with information to steer and support your movement into the future.

- What may become possible because you make this choice?
- What actions will you take to bring your choice to life?

To make it easier to work through these big questions without feeling overwhelmed, I've laid out the steps for finding your answers in the table on page 154. Each question is broken down into manageable, specific actions to take to find answers, forming a framework that is designed to gradually guide you into your future choice.

The Framework for Making a Future Choice

Chapter

What may become possible as you make your choice?   21

  ✳ Connect to possibility through continued inquiry and an ongoing question-and-answer dialogue with yourself

  ✳ Identify and shift limiting beliefs that could hold you back

What actions will you take to bring your choice to life?   22

  ✳ Take small, imperfect steps toward what matters to build momentum

  ✳ Say yes and develop trust that you can handle what arises

What unfolds from your action?   23

  ✳ Pause after you take action to allow for unfolding and the ripple effect to take hold

---

In the chapters to come, I'll explain each part of this approach to making a future choice. I'll pose the questions and then provide examples of the subtleties of how my clients and I have answered them.

CHAPTER 21

Connecting to Possibility

Fear and possibility straddle opposite sides of a map and opposite sides of the emotional spectrum. When your fear level is high, your choice must matter significantly enough to pull you through it. As heavily-weighted fear branches become dwarfed by those that bloom with possibility, the words and emotions you've envisioned draw you into the future toward the allure of future promise.

When you want something in the distance but simultaneously feel caught between the worlds of "what was" and "what will be," you're sitting in a liminal space.

It can be difficult and painful to tolerate uncertainty when the route to what you want still feels ethereal.

It's challenging to discern how to get where you want to go. What does it take to manage the discomfort of a choice yet unrealized? What's the key to enduring frustration until you establish your path?

The key is to focus on what's possible for you.

To connect with possibility, let's concentrate on the Exploration Map question: **What may become possible because you make this choice?**

While the answers to this question fuel momentum, the inherent largeness in considering what's possible can feel overwhelming. To avoid this "freeze" response, my suggestion is to take a first pass at answering this question on your own. Find a quiet spot, light a candle, take some deep breaths and visualize yourself days and weeks into the future. Flesh out ideas of your potential from a joyful, curious space. Then enlist the support of someone you trust who will likely see greater possibilities for you. Ask them to imagine you stepping into your choice, and share what they see as possible. So often the trusted people in our lives see more of our untapped potential than we can for ourselves.

As you reflect on the question of possibility, you'll first speculate about what's possible, specifically for you. Then, if appropriate to your choice, consider expanding your inquiry.

- What's possible for your clients and your business?
- What's possible for those close to you?
- What's possible for the world at large?

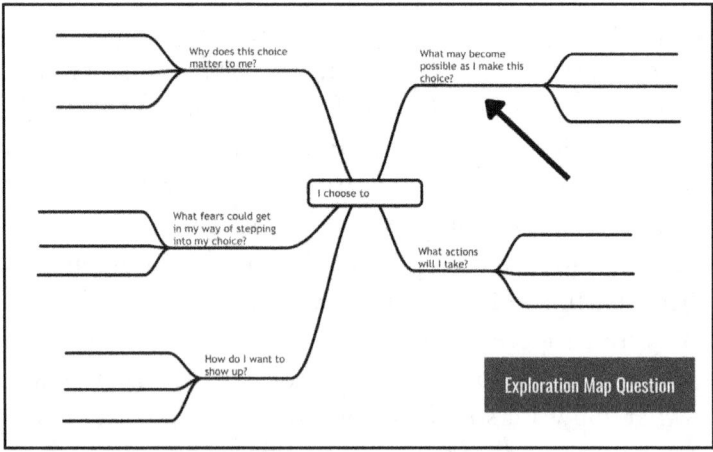

Possibilty in Action

While writing this section, I approached a meaningful crossroads: Would I step away from lucrative consulting into the unknown and pursue my dreams of applying all I'd learned and processed related to choice?

My question wasn't exactly would I, but *when* would I?

By brainstorming what might be possible, not focusing on or worrying about when it would happen, my map began to stretch into the future, further into possibility, outside the scope of what I'd previously imagined. The more I connected with my desire to do something meaningful and purposeful that would make the most of my gifts, the more I realized that what I wanted was more expansive than I'd imagined. I knew, deep-in-my-gut knew, that I must take steps toward possibility.

The following stories illustrate how two clients navigated agonizing times, ultimately focusing on what was possible, which served as a guiding light to persevere.

Possibility Choice 1

My long-standing client, Lori, experienced several claustrophobic moments during quarantine and felt as though she was suffocating. Needing help to manage her anxiety and wanting to reinvigorate her life and spirit with levity, she contemplated working with a new therapist. Together, we documented all she wanted to accomplish to shift her thoughts and behaviors, while addressing what could undermine her best intentions.

Her map began with: *I choose to consider working with a new therapist.*

Note how adding the word "consider" softens the choice of "I choose to work with a new therapist" by adding breathing room to navigate a choice that feels meaningful but may generate feelings of conflict.

To illustrate the challenge of determining what's possible, let me share a summary of how Lori addressed each of the map's exploration questions before settling on what she determined was possible.

For each reason she documented as to why this choice mattered to her, she felt an equally valid fear associated with it.

- She wanted help but feared taking the necessary actions.

- She wanted support in overcoming stagnancy and anguish but was reluctant to admit the depth of her pain and have a stranger witness the truth of her darkness.

- She wanted assistance dissecting the monotony of her stories to assess what was truth and what she'd grown beyond, yet she vacillated between whether she wanted accountability or not, and questioned if a new therapist would push her to go deeper than she could on her own.

Noting the roadblocks she'd erected to beginning therapy, she could see that fear impeded her progress. To move through this emotion, she'd need to strongly connect to what was possible.

- What would it take to get the most out of her therapy experience?
- How would she promise to show up with a new therapist?
- What actions would she take as she resumed treatment?
- What would become possible for her after doing the work?

To make her time in therapy worthwhile, she'd have to revise obsolete stories and be amenable to new ways of communicating. Although this felt like a high bar to reach in her current state, the prospect of adopting new behaviors and attitudes was appealing after having felt stifled for nearly a year.

What would become possible by working with a new therapist?

- With new perspectives and insights, she would shift her stories so that she felt lighter and brought more levity into her life.
- Her anxiety would be tempered with tools she developed.

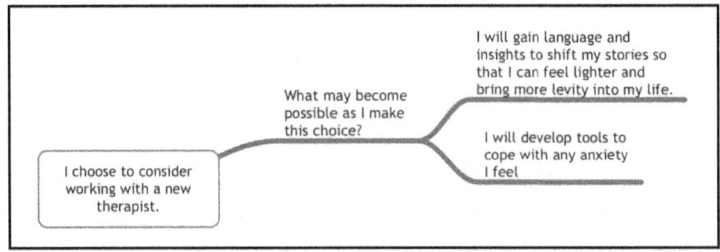

With a deeper understanding into why she was making this choice, and what it would take to fully commit, a spark of hope arose and the scales tipped from fear to possibility.

Connecting with possibility was the missing ingredient Lori needed. Seeing what was possible laid out across the page encouraged her to move from considering working with a new therapist to actually saying yes.

Possibilities can be short-term visions of how you want to feel or more grandiose visions of what you want to manifest. By creating a map documenting your thoughts, you're preserving your ideas of what's possible to revisit should roadblocks re-emerge.

Possibility Choice 2

Allison, a single mom in her mid-forties, had grown emotionally depleted as she navigated big areas of her life alone: uncomfortable interactions with her ex-husband, client demands, concern about her health, anxiety regarding her finances, and continued stress and nervousness about how her children were dealing with modern life.

Even though each challenge on its own was debilitating, being alone without companionship affected her most acutely. While she had a desire to cultivate a loving relationship, she felt ambivalence, wanting, yet also not wanting, partnership.

Like Lori, Allison softened the intensity of her choice by adding the word "consider" and began her map with: *I choose to consider opening myself up to find a loving relationship.*

She longed for touch but equally craved solitude. She wanted a man who embraced everything about who she is, but having lost her mother to dementia and witnessing her disappearance, she suspected her mother's ailment might befall her. She future-feared: *Will what happened to my mother happen to me? And, if so, will I allow anyone to care for me? And, if I did, would they want to? And, if they did, what would it take to let someone into that vulnerable space?*

Each fear-based question served as a barrier to hide behind, providing a convenient rationalization to stay rooted in what was familiar. Unraveling each question's specificity allowed her to get beyond the panic cycle to a more rational space, and to admit she wanted to live in the moment and not fear the future.

What would become possible as she opened herself to finding love?

- She might meet someone who could become a true life partner.
- She might meet someone who could understand and console her.
- She might meet someone who would bring great joy into her life.

Holding onto positive thoughts about what would be possible, she made the decision to move forth with her choice and take a courageous leap to shift her life to one she desired. (See her map on the following page.)

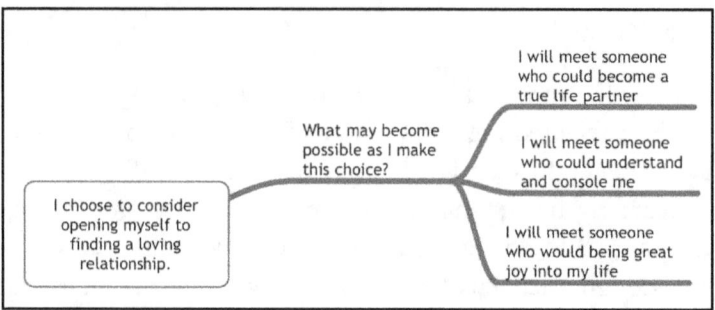

Shifting Limiting Beliefs

Limiting beliefs are the debris of past invalidating experiences. Like rubble in the road, they block your way forward, causing paralysis and stagnation and inhibiting you from getting what you want. They thwart your efforts to make the personal, professional and relationship choices that matter to you.

Unlike rubble, limiting beliefs are not physical obstacles—they are ephemeral roadblocks. Since they're not easy to see, it's natural to think your limiting beliefs are true even when they aren't. Similar to your fears, it's essential to assess which disempowering beliefs are tethering you to the past, hindering you from making the choice you desire. Mapping can support you to dissect the details of your belief—what the belief actually is, where it originated, and how you may shift it to one that's more encouraging so you can move forward.

Limiting beliefs hamper your ability to see what's possible. As you connect to possibility in this section, one way to find the most expansive potential is to consider, **what *limiting beliefs could hold you back from making this choice?***

In the following examples, I'll share how clients have worked through limiting beliefs around relationships, business and health.

Limiting Belief 1

After three marriages, my client Andrea dreamt of being in a loving relationship but had grown doubtful of its possibility. As a kind and attentive man demonstrated interest, the traumas and hurt she'd endured from previous relationships acted as handcuffs, shackling her to the past, precluding her from entering the world she knew she wanted.

She felt resistant to opening herself to him, anxious she'd be mistreated. What if he cheated? What if he left her? What if he wasn't who she thought he was?

"Let me ask you this," I questioned directly. "Do you want to live in a place of doubt and apprehension that any future man will hurt you because of his unaddressed baggage? Or, are you ready to let go of the limiting belief that all men are bad?"

"I want to let that belief go, but it's so ingrained in my psyche due to past experiences that I don't know how to do that," she confided.

Change starts with a subtle shift in your thinking, an acknowledgment that your old ways and thoughts are holding you back, causing a self-fulfilling prophecy you'll continually recreate until you change your thoughts.

As you see yourself reaching for a choice, but notice you're experiencing resistance, state definitively what you're choosing. For Andrea, it was: *I choose to be in a beautiful and loving relationship.*

Then continue with questions to drill down and understand:

- What is holding you back from stepping into this choice that matters to you?
- What limiting belief is affecting your forward movement?
- Where does that belief come from?
- What will it take to rewrite it as a new and supportive belief?

Below is one leg of Andrea's map showing how these questions guided her investigation.

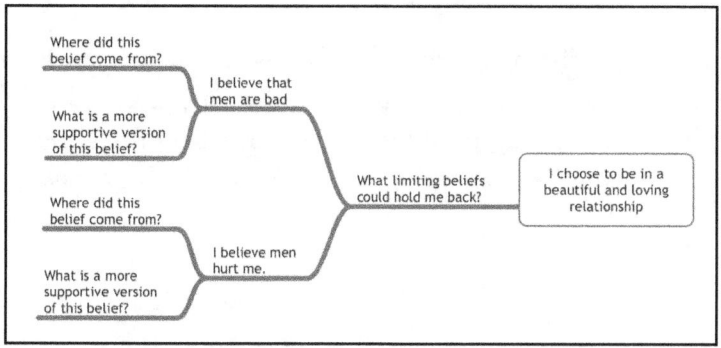

Like Andrea, you may have a strong desire to step into something new, but have fears and beliefs to overcome before you take the plunge. When feelings of depression, sadness and lethargy crop up, let those emotions be a cue to notice your resistance. Have an internal dialogue with yourself and ask: *What unsupportive limiting beliefs are filling my thoughts?*

Consider asking a friend to help you transform your thoughts from those that hinder you to those that serve you. What would someone who loves you believe is possible for you, and what would it take to have that vision for yourself?

You can use a map to capture your questions and responses. As you can see from Andrea's example, the map structure supports and organizes continued questioning.

Limiting Belief 2

Kathleen dreamt of starting a coaching practice to share her healing experience after enduring years of chronic pain. She wanted freedom to make money running her business her way. Having always worked for others, she harbored a number of disempowering beliefs related to marketing, her vulnerability and timing that interfered with her dream.

- I should have done this sooner.
- Trained therapists are better at this work than I am.
- Marketing is hard. I'll never be able to find clients on my own.
- The longer I don't do this, the less capable I am to do it.
- I'll get hurt if clients reject me.

Identifying a disempowering belief allows you to inspect it with an adult perspective and reframe it to become supportive and encouraging. For example, Kathleen subtly shifted her belief of *the longer I don't do this, the less capable I am to do it* to *the sooner I do this, the more people I will help.*

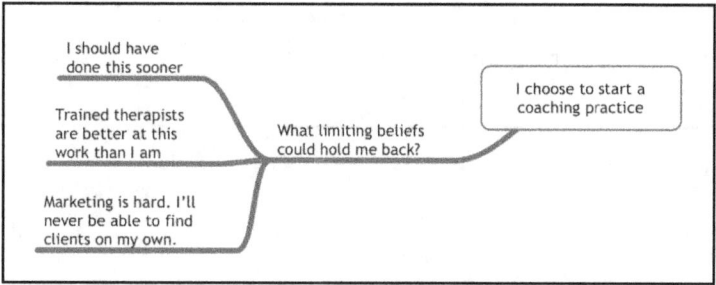

Limiting Belief 3

When Serena was diagnosed with ADD and learning disabilities at the age of five, her parents treated her with kid gloves, not wanting to add to the pressure of a diagnosis they were ill-equipped to handle. Unlike her brother, who they repeatedly pushed to do more, Serena received the feedback that she was "dense" and constantly encouraged: "You're doing great, that's the best you can do."

Having battled insomnia since high school, she'd grown moody, volatile and explosive in her thirties. Being afraid and frustrated her entire life, she often felt insecure and incapable of traveling without worries.

Her medication affected her memory which triggered anxiety of familial dementia. After experimenting with supplements, medications, healers and alternative treatments, she was determined to uncover the root cause of her illness so it no longer affected her emotional well-being.

As a starting point, she identified a few core limiting beliefs she was prepared to address:

- Nighttime scares me as I never sleep easily.
- I am fragile.
- I can't do activities that others can.

Contemplating these declarations, so dramatically stated, she connected with the childlike energy they contained. As she grew to understand her emotions more deeply, she grasped the link between her adult feelings and the way she'd been treated in her youth. To begin overcoming these outdated beliefs, Serena would recall past choices that highlighted her strengths and actively seek opportunities to demonstrate her capabilities.

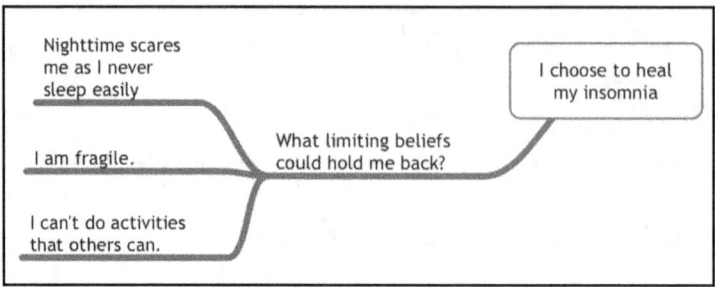

Many limiting beliefs are internalized from childhood and appear to be as irrefutable as the sky being blue and grass being green. Take time to reflect upon any beliefs that have prevented you from achieving what you want. As you expose them, appreciate how they've influenced your actions and ideas of what's possible.

By shifting the energy of your negative thoughts into language that's more uplifting, you'll construct an arsenal of positive beliefs to have readily on hand so you don't get held back by what may have gotten in your way in the past.

CHAPTER 22

Creating Momentum Through Action

So far, we've covered two of the five components in the framework of making a future choice:

The Framework for Making a Future Choice

	Chapter

What may become possible as you make your choice?   21

✳ Connect to possibility through continued inquiry and an ongoing question-and-answer dialogue with yourself

✳ Identify and shift limiting beliefs that could hold you back

What actions will you take to bring your choice to life?   22

✳ Take small, imperfect steps toward what matters to build momentum

✳ Say yes and develop trust that you can handle what arises

What unfolds from your action?   23

✳ Pause after you take action to allow for unfolding and the ripple effect to take hold

The next step is to take action.

A choice is beginning-focused and a springboard from which you take action. A choice is a place you're starting, which is distinct from a goal—a place you're going. Taking action toward a small, proactive choice instantly creates movement and energy that ripples outward.

Our lives are typically not altered by giant leaps but by small steps which lead to more significant transformation. The benefit of making a choice and then taking action is the momentum it generates, which acts as an unseen force bringing the unexpected into your life.

Taking one action, however small and modest, removes the pressure of knowing each detail required to make your choice a reality. With an awareness of momentum principles, you create the way forward as you go. Just as you can drive on a foggy night with the visibility of your dim lights shining a few feet in front of you, you can walk onto the path of your choice with consciousness and presence, seeing a glimmer one step ahead, allowing momentum to support you along the way.

As you create your map and ask yourself the Exploration Map question **what action will you take?**, my recommendation is to select a manageable, short-term action that feels doable and gives you a sense of agency toward bringing your choice to fruition.

Each morning, and anytime you're feeling stuck, you have the opportunity to jumpstart your day by making a new choice and then taking a corresponding small action. You can choose to reestablish healthy habits and take the action of drinking a green juice in the morning or getting up thirty minutes early to do something that matters to you. You can choose to connect with old friends and take the action to reach out to someone you haven't spoken to for a while. Once you've made a choice, action ignites momentum.

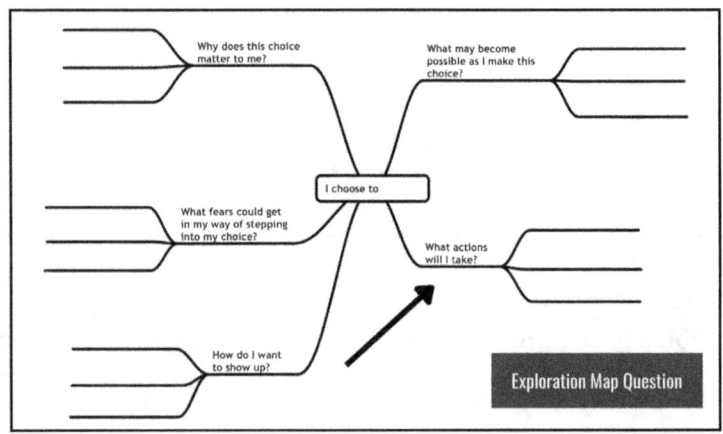

In the following examples, three clients demonstrate how simple actions supported the forward momentum for a relationship choice, a personal choice and a professional choice.

Andrea, who I mentioned earlier regarding her struggle with unsupportive beliefs about men, chose to be in a beautiful and loving relationship. She committed to taking two key actions. First, she vowed that in her next therapy session, she'd request support to address the root of her limiting beliefs which were preventing her from getting what she wanted. She'd ask her therapist for language to shift her beliefs so they would tell a story of hope versus fear. With her beliefs adjusted, she'd take the plunge into the dating world and update her online dating profile to better represent who she is and what she wants in a relationship.

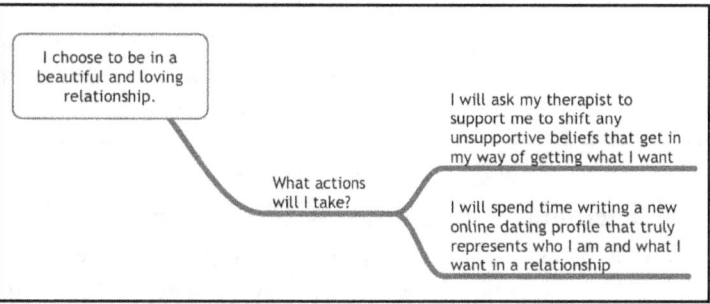

Lea was burnt out being a corporate attorney. She hadn't enforced professional boundaries and was exhausted by legal demands that infiltrated all aspects of her existence. She was ready to bring more fun into her life. Assessing the actions she'd take, she pledged that she'd carve out a few hours each week from her calendar to add three activities that felt like fun. To eliminate tasks that drained her, like cleaning her house, she'd hire a housekeeper.

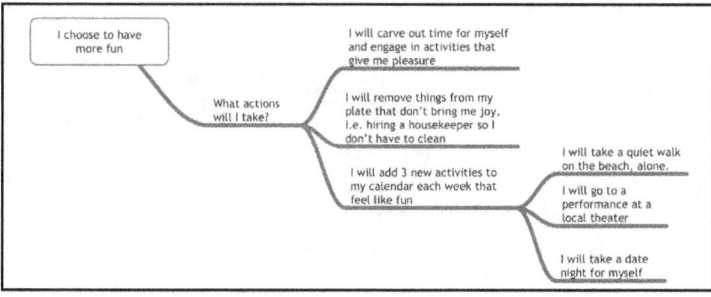

Brenda had been a coach for two years but had never received money for her services. Ready to take her business from pro bono to paid, but nervous to make this leap, she committed to her first action of opening a business bank account so she'd be prepared to receive money. Next, to make booking sessions easier for her paying clients, she'd add a scheduling tool to her website. Finally, knowing she needed to have the difficult conversations with her existing pro bono clients, she would prepare a script inviting each to become a paid client.

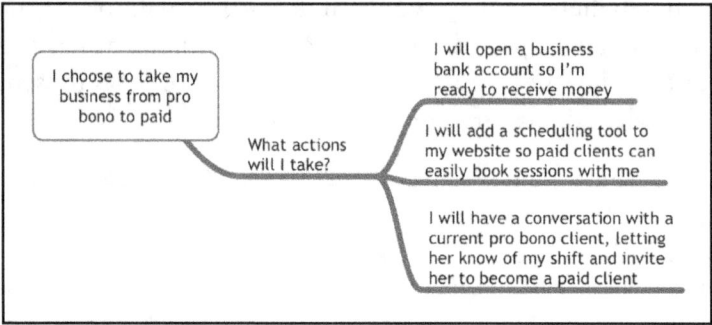

As you determine the actions you'll take to move your choice forward, create two legs in your map, one that represents those actions you'd like to do in the short term (within the next week or month) and those within a longer timeframe.

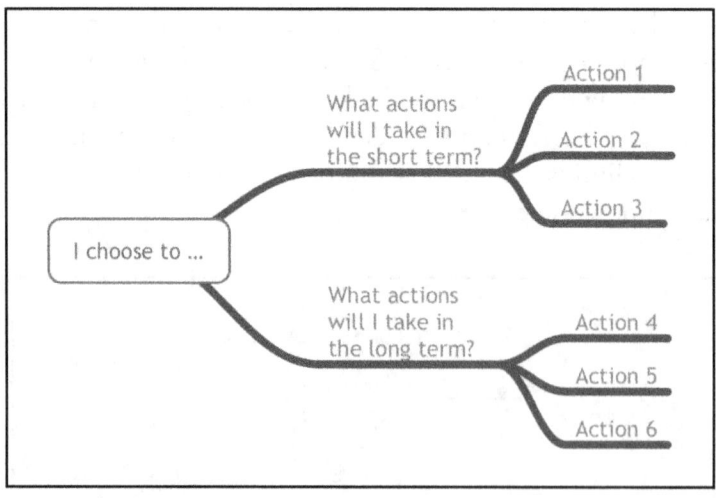

Taking Small Imperfect Action

The choices we make are seldom black or white, good or bad. Choices have layers of complexity embedded within them, so there is rarely a perfect choice, only the perfect choice for you at this moment.

Ideally, each proactive choice would be an intentional and conscious commitment to do something that matters to you. There may be times however, when you may have to make an interim decision, one that feels good enough for now. Taking this action may not align perfectly with your original choice, but it represents a step forward.

Let me share some examples of what making a smaller choice can look like.

In a short window of time, three friends reached out for relationship advice as they tolerated unmet expectations. Each was in a challenging partnership, but none was prepared to leave. In our conversations, we addressed a smaller component of their choice and picked a more specific and manageable component on which to focus.

Small Imperfect Action 1

Gina adored the man she was dating, but knew that due to his idiosyncrasies and their incompatibilities he wasn't her forever person. While she wasn't ready to leave, she incessantly questioned if staying was in her best interest.

I suggested she put that larger choice of *I choose to leave my relationship* aside and instead focus on one smaller in scale.

"What if you choose to stay in the imperfection of the relationship for a time?" I proposed. "What if you could accept that while the relationship is not all you want, part of it is, and that's okay. Since you're not prepared to leave him, can you choose to enjoy what you have for a time and not get mired in the relationship's longevity?"

"That feels much more realistic and less stressful," she expressed.

Small Imperfect Action 2

Callie often complained about what she lacked with her husband and nagged him continually about her unmet expectations. While he was a loving father and close friend, their marriage was strained and lacked the intimacy she craved. As her sixteen-year old daughter struggled with medical and emotional challenges, Callie deliberated if divorcing at this juncture was too burdensome for her child.

"Do you need to make the big choice about divorce now?" I questioned. "Divorce is never a perfect decision, and there's undoubtedly no perfection to its timing. Instead of focusing on the disappointment of what you don't have, what about putting your relationship aspirations on pause to support your daughter to navigate the balance of her high school years?"

When I presented the option of consciously staying in the imperfection of the relationship, each friend exhaled the weight in relief. Each felt like she was granted permission to not make a big decision that didn't feel right in the moment, but could instead move forward with a smaller choice that felt more manageable and take actions accordingly.

The smaller choice was an option neither had considered. Ambivalence and indecision had left each feeling deadlocked. Now, making a smaller choice with intentionality shifted the terrain. Both friends could see new opportunities and routes forward.

Small Imperfect Action 3

Days later, my friend Suzy, a pediatrician, lamented that she no longer felt aligned with the physicians in her office and was growing frustrated with the medical group's professional dynamics, politics and corporate structure.

After the consecutive losses of her father and close friend, her partners lacked compassion for her need to take time off to grieve. Their insensitivity led her to question their humanity, and to feel it wasn't healthy to remain in business with them.

"Are you prepared to walk away from the practice?" I questioned.

Suzy emphatically declared no.

"Then what smaller choice feels best to make now based on wanting to stay?" I asked.

"My highest priority is to be fully present with my patients, so my smaller choice is to do my inner healing privately so I can wholeheartedly serve them."

In a perfect world, each choice would feel glorious, but to foster momentum you must sometimes make a smaller choice, one that feels satisfactory. Scaling back the breadth of a choice can temper your anxiety while still allowing you to move forward. Smaller adjustments can have a meaningful impact in the face of a large problem.

Instead of standing paralyzed when big choices feel overwhelming or unreachable, honing in on a smaller choice generates forward motion. Taking action, however small, stirs things up and allows for momentum to bring you forward or guide you in a direction you never would have expected.

Saying Yes

One of the most straightforward ways to create momentum through action is choosing to say yes, especially when you feel uncertain. Stretching beyond what's comfortable actively challenges your fears and limiting beliefs, and allows you to notice that you're more courageous and capable than you originally thought.

Saying yes is expansive. It's about what can be. It evokes possibility. As you open yourself to saying yes to anything that sparks your interest, you demonstrate enthusiasm for your life.

One cold wintry morning I chose to attend a yoga class when I hadn't gone in months. Though my brain cited many reasons to stay inside, I sensed this decision held greater significance than merely taking a class or not.

I knew being on my mat in the yoga studio's zen would clear my head. I knew flowing through the poses would provide my body with movement it craved. I trusted being in a space other than my home would allow fresh thoughts and ideas to flow more freely. Sensing these possibilities and feeling eager to welcome them in, I chose to go to yoga. My intentional yes to yoga was an even more significant yes to momentum, to movement and to what it could open up for me.

As you consider making a future choice, you might feel resistant to saying yes because you feel tentative, particularly if you've never done what you're saying yes to. When these moments arise, saying yes can be an exercise in building trust that you can handle whatever comes your way. Instead of waiting to jump in when you're sure of what you're doing, believe you can say yes whenever you feel moved to, knowing you'll find answers as you need them.

Here are a few personal examples of what's happened when I've felt called to say yes.

Saying Yes 1

The year in which I created my first twenty-nine maps coincided with the year I began immersing myself in the teachings and spiritual practice of Kabbalah. Hungering for depth of connection and eager to improve the dynamics of how I showed up in relationships, I digitally digested reverential wisdom and principles to raise my level of consciousness.

Nudging me to experience the spiritual practice through more connected interaction, my mentor encouraged me to join the Kabbalah community in person. "There's a Rosh Hashanah service coming up in San Diego and I recommend you go."

I internally debated: Did I want to travel, did I want to spend the money, was it worth it, did I care?

"This is an important next step for you, Kim. Don't worry about the details you're questioning; just jump and trust," he firmly suggested.

Upon waking the next morning, I said yes.

Within moments of arriving at the event, a woman asked, "Who did you come with?"

"I came alone." I stated with nervous excitement. Taken aback, she asked, "Are you telling me you traveled across the country by yourself to attend an event with over 4,000 people?"

"Yes, does that seem strange to you?" I questioned.

"It'd be impossible for me to do it," she admitted, "but I commend you for having that courage. Let me introduce you to the people in my community."

And, all because I said yes, I was welcomed in.

Saying Yes 2

The act of saying yes changes your internal state, allowing joy to emanate from within.

During a conversation with a good friend, she shared, "We're going to Italy and our dog sitter just canceled."

"Would you like me to care for her?" I offered.

"Are you sure?" she asked quizzically.

"Yes, it'd be fun."

"Do you need to think about it?" she asked quizzically again.

"No, I thought about it. I'm saying yes."

And with my simple choice of saying yes, made using fun as my filter, a delicious Bernese Mountain dog entered my home to receive a month of love. We walked a quiet trail each morning, I unplugged periodically throughout the day to relish petting her soft fur, and my kids felt a renewed sense of excitement being at home with her gentle presence.

The simple yes of a new choice is a tool that is always at your disposal to shift your disposition. You can bring more fun, connection or laughter into your life by choosing to seek it out.

Saying Yes 3

A few summers back, I was in a depressive slump. I felt overwhelmed with the weight of how my father's degeneration from Alzheimer's was affecting our family. I felt saddened by the emotional challenges my daughter was experiencing. I felt professionally bereft and unfulfilled, and I'd succumbed to the melancholy of being without a partner.

After dropping my daughter off at her summer program, I pulled over for a much-needed cry. I was tired of responding to "how are you?" with the gravity of my circumstances. I was tired of feeling weighed down. I craved moments of lightness in the midst of my heaviness, and in the quiet of my car made the choice to act as if I felt joy before I actually experienced it.

Saying yes to joy didn't mean masking my sadness or denying the reality of my life's circumstances. Instead, it meant intentionally seeking opportunities that brought me happiness, trusting that I could experience moments of beauty even during difficult times. I focused my energy on connecting deeply with others, which always recalibrates my demeanor. I spent time feeling grateful for what was present in my life and engaged in activities that made me happy. I trusted that taking the small action of readily saying yes would set the stage for a shift to occur, leading to movement I could not yet see.

I said yes to hosting a women's gathering and found joy in deciding who I'd invite, what food I'd prepare, how I'd make my home more welcoming and the anticipation of our interesting conversations. My rejuvenated energy and shift in attitude allowed me to move through my malaise and stop wallowing in my depressive thoughts.

Saying Yes 4

There's great value in saying yes with the confidence that your yes will lead to something worthwhile.

After sharing my first map with my friend Nancy, her next six words surprised and invigorated me: "Would you do one for me?"

Although I'd never created a map for someone else, I said yes immediately and eagerly, feeling confident it would be a special experience for us both. Despite having no tangible method, I trusted that if I connected with her deeply, allowed myself to be guided by the answers to her questions, and listened intently, I'd provide her with a valuable experience. I asked her to come to our call with the answer to one question: What choice in her life would she like to explore?

From one question and our deep dive conversation, my method's birthing process began, and everything that you've read in this book is a result of having said yes to Nancy's request. This first yes, a moment of trusting myself to figure out a way even when I wasn't certain of exactly how to proceed, allowed me to experience the magic of what could be. That feeling of promise fueled many more yeses in the nine years of writing this book.

The act of saying yes to something intriguing and then figuring out the details later builds trust and self-confidence. Trust is knowing that even when you can't predict what's next, you can handle whatever comes your way. Trust is built by going beyond what's comfortable and acknowledging that you're capable of handling more than you imagined.

If you don't know the answer, you can find it. If something difficult happens, you can cope. If what you're moving toward continues to feel like a yes, take the next step. If there's a shift and your gut rumbles with confusion, pause and make a new choice to course-correct.

The act of moving forward through these steps will carry you to the other side of your uncertainty. You can pause for the purpose of considering your next step, but step you must, even if it's a tiny one. As you move into your chosen future and build trust in yourself, you'll find a lightness and opening of paths ahead that exceeds what you'd previously envisioned.

CHAPTER 23

Allowing the Future to Unfold

We've now covered four of five components in the framework of making a future choice:

The Framework for Making a Future Choice	Chapter
What may become possible as you make your choice?	21
✳ Connect to possibility through continued inquiry and an ongoing question-and-answer dialogue with yourself	
✳ Identify and shift limiting beliefs that could hold you back	
What actions will you take to bring your choice to life?	22
✳ Take small, imperfect steps toward what matters to build momentum	
✳ Say yes and develop trust that you can handle what arises	
What unfolds from your action?	23
✳ Pause after you take action to allow for unfolding and the ripple effect to take hold	

Now, the final step is to pause to **allow for unfolding** and the ripple effect.

Pause to Notice Unfolding

As you proceed confidently onto the path of your choice, two worlds move in tandem. One, the world of action. The other, the world of unfolding. As you nurture your choice through purposeful action, it's essential to pause to notice the unexpected gems of synchronicity and opportunity that organically present themselves.

In the world of action, you take the necessary steps to bring your choice to life, drawing on masculine, doing energy. In the world of unfolding, you intentionally pause and exert no energy—the present unravels instead of being forcefully shaped. The feminine nature of unfolding invites you to sit in an observational place of uncertainty, to surrender control and notice with openness what comes toward you. Unfolding encourages you to be receptive to new thoughts, people, opportunities and encounters that materialize. Unfolding is not about *making* anything happen; it's about watching what happens naturally because of choices and changes you've decided to make. In the space of unfolding, your most important tool is your surrender, not your to-do list.

As a teenager, my daughter was interested in fashion and took classes designing, creating and sewing her own clothes. She wasn't sure about her future and didn't know if fashion would be or should be a part of it.

"You don't need to know that now," I explained to her. "Just keep taking action on what interests you at the moment and see where it goes. By taking action, things will open up for you. You may love a teacher who guides you to another class. You may have an internship opportunity that will show you something you love or don't love about fashion. Regardless, you'll have information because you took action and things opened up. Whether you choose to follow the openings becomes another choice."

Unfolding means you allow something to happen to you, not in a victim-like way, but that you leave yourself open to forces outside of your influence.

With the busy-ness of life, it's easy to overlook the unfolding accessible to you with each choice. Your actions set in motion possibilities that are beyond your control. The X factor, alchemical spark, the stroke of luck that causes people, experiences and opportunities you likely didn't predict or imagine to show up seemingly out of the ethers. Once you realize that this magic is always available to you and hone your senses to notice its subtle footprints, you can appreciate the richness that lies before you at any given moment. Suddenly, choice is not solely about action and the burden of getting things done which rests heavily on your shoulders. Instead, each action is fodder for transformation, welcoming opportunities to appear that defy your planning or expectation.

Having a heightened sense of awareness as you move through your life affords you the opportunity to observe and pay attention to what's occurring. When you pause to notice what happened because of your choice, both due to your deliberate action and the unfolding which occurs outside your control, you can appreciate the richness of the journey you're on and witness the abundance and support that's shown up. Just as keeping a gratitude journal allows you to notice the gifts present in your everyday life, recognizing what's expanding as a result of your choices invites further growth.

What happened because you began moving and taking action? What other choices are presenting themselves to you because you made an initial choice?

There is balance in taking action while also watching for what organically unfolds. By paying attention to both realms, you sense the full spectrum of what's available to you.

Before having the vision for this book, I did not have the sensitivity to notice anything unfolding; my focus was exclusively on action. It wasn't until I shared my initial map with my friend Nancy, who knew me as the "Get It Done Girl," that my perception changed.

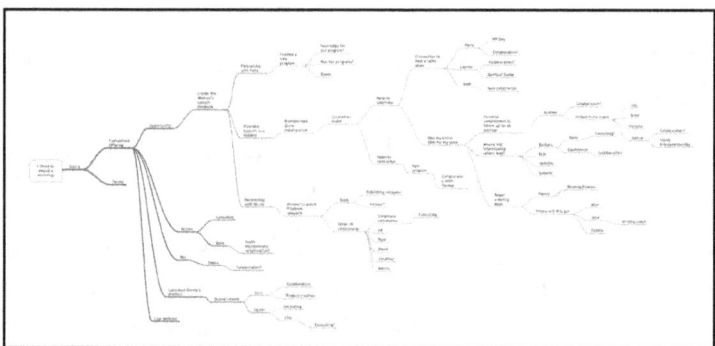

Observing the many branches spanning the width of my first map's page, noting the momentum I'd created from one choice, Nancy interjected to say, "Kim, you're in a rich birthing place with these maps, and while I know you want to take charge and jump into implementer mode, can I suggest you let this mapping part of your life evolve? Can you have faith it will unfold? Can you let it birth without knowing where it's going to lead and what may come from it?"

Her request was unprecedented and altogether surreal—she was proposing that I stop my drug of choice (aka doing) and consider staying metaphorically pregnant in a part of my life, not knowing what might emerge.

Contemplating her beautiful request, which both scared and thrilled me as I'd never consciously chosen to sit in a space of uncertainty, I gave myself permission to revel in the unknown of exploring choices and creating maps for others without worrying about any outcomes.

During my immersive year of mapping, engaged in numerous deep-dive discovery conversations, thoughts filled my head as to what I might do with all I was capturing, synthesizing and learning. What was possible?

- Might I share the stories in a book?

- Might I use the information gathered in creating a map as an assessment for new coaching clients?

- Might I teach others how to examine their choices using a mapping tool?

- Would I invent a live mapping app that could display the unfolding of current choices?

- Might I create an art exhibit of life atlases of past, present and future choices?

- Would I speak to young people and encourage them to have greater awareness about the power of their choices?

I captured each of my ideas in a map (of course) but took no action. I allowed my thoughts to flow with possibility, knowing for a time I'd do nothing but let more and more unfold. Using a map to preserve my ideas, trusting they were held in a safe and treasured space, relieved me of the pressure of needing to take immediate action.

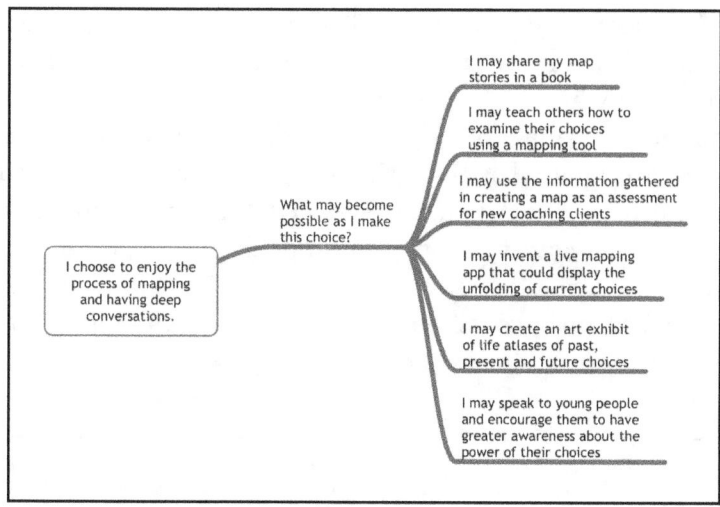

In a gestation phase, you may feel uneasy not knowing where your choice will lead. Using an Unfolding Map, you can document the people, opportunities, thoughts and experiences presenting themselves that without your attention might otherwise go unnoticed.

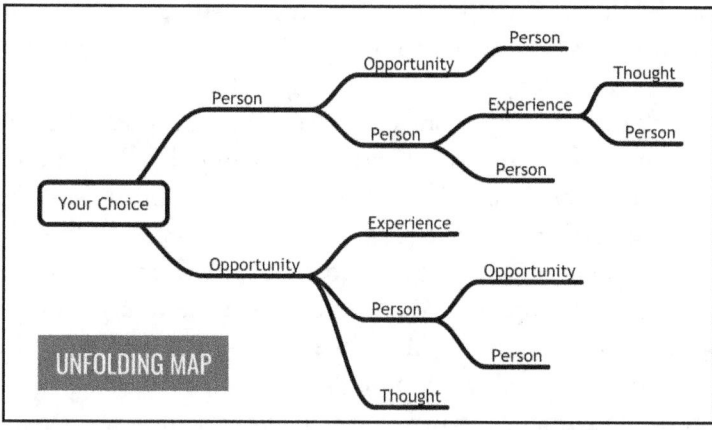

Imagine being invited to participate in an exciting project that intrigues you but about which you know little. Choosing to say yes, you take action to attend an informational meeting. What might be asked of you? What might you learn? Who might you meet? What new interests might you explore? Where else may you be guided?

As I developed an awareness of what was unfolding rather than concentrating solely on action, I began to make choices with an excitement for what might transpire.

Choosing to bring more joy into my life, I spent an afternoon at an urban loft visiting local artists. Drawn to the magnetic and welcoming nature of an artist who designed mixed media creative journals, I shared my vision of making my maps three-dimensional. Our conversation opened the floodgate for additional brainstorming, and culminated in the ideas to co-lead a workshop integrating choice and journaling, and for me to develop a painting practice.

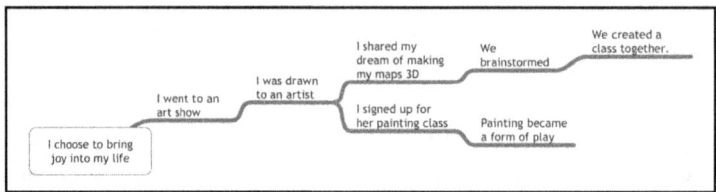

Wanting to step away from my computer and bring my message about choice into greater visibility, a good friend nudged me to begin speaking. I fully invested in myself, and my words, by spending fifty hours crafting an outline that would be the framework for a twenty-minute presentation. Visualizing that these short talks would be the foundation for my soon-to-be TED Talk, I expressed confidence in my future. In the months before the pandemic, I followed every lead and spoke wherever I got an invitation—corporate breakfasts, women's business meetings and after-hours networking events. As momentum built and my energy generated more energy, a friend from my past, who I'd not connected with for more than a decade, invited me to speak at her women's community luncheon. The unfolding continued. (See my map on the following page.)

Until I began mapping my own personal journey and then diving deep with others, I never realized how powerful each choice has the potential to be. Maintaining awareness of your choices while immersed in a multitude of tasks can be challenging. When you're busy and distracted, you miss connecting the dots between the experiences and opportunities that unfold in that space.

There is magic to what unfolds beyond what is apparent. In addition to creating momentum, making one small, proactive choice can unleash possibilities that go beyond what you could have imagined—

from something seemingly small, a great deal can emerge. Having the openness to digress from your linear path toward a beckoning diversion can enrich and expand your life's experience.

By releasing the need to focus on your end destination, you can revel in detours and immerse yourself in a meandering, and often more meaningful journey.

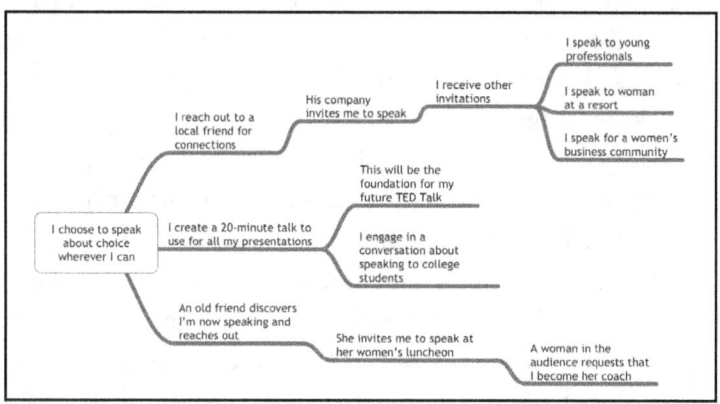

The Ripple Effect

Unfolding reflects how choices affect *your* life. When you make a choice and then take action, you also create a ripple that spreads into the lives of others.

Each choice, like an accurately positioned stone skimming across the calm waters of a lake, causes a ripple of unknown possibilities and opportunities by creating movement from stillness. Your choices can and do lead to ripple effects, whether you notice them or not. Who may you influence? Who may you impact?

Your small choices and the actions you take have the power to influence others in ways you can't begin to imagine.

Shortly after I began noticing everything we do through the lens of choice, I awoke at two in the morning to find the TED Talk of a mom named Robyn O'Brien, who, like many unsuspecting moms, didn't know what was in the food she fed her children. "I grew up eating Doritos and Twinkies. I fed my four kids whatever I got at the store, but it wasn't until my youngest daughter had an allergic reaction to something she ate that I went on a mission to understand what's in our food and what's changed since we were kids."

To find out why her child was allergic to food, she chose to become a detective, searching out whether there was something in milk, corn and food proteins that wasn't there when we were kids. How were the food conglomerates using these chemically engineered changes to maximize their profits? Was there an association between food modification and cancer rates?

Her growing knowledge, coupled with the disturbing facts she uncovered, led her to become an activist. While she didn't intend to become a crusader for cleaning up the food supply, as she shared her newfound knowledge with other parents, she became the Erin Brockovich of the food industry. One mom, who made one choice, created a ripple effect of industry change and information for others.

Robyn's choice to do something that mattered ultimately influenced many, including me. In the darkness and solitude of the night, I felt an internal bubbling; I wanted to learn more about others who made choices that made a difference and led to something unexpected on the other side. I wanted to understand what drove their choices and what became possible as a result. I asked friends for connections and watched with excitement as links to interesting TED Talks began populating my inbox.

One woman chose to ride an elephant a thousand miles across India. One celebrity chose to give gifts to her fans. One man chose to take a different route to work.

The videos kept coming—stories of people who'd made a choice that grew beyond them.

Feeling called to be a messenger dispensing stories of seemingly small yet incredibly impactful choices, I envisioned using my gift of connecting easily, combined with my love of deep and curious inquiry, to delve into the meaningful choices of others, to understand their process, what inspired their choice, and what came of their actions so I could share their journey.

My inner knowing led me to create a podcast called *The Voice of Choice* that allowed me to learn more about amazing everyday people who made a choice that created a ripple of positive influence in their lives and the lives of others. Without any guarantee as to what would come of my idea, I innately understood that moving forward with my podcast was an essential and inspired project—a choice to which I must say yes.

I imagined people across all demographics taking in diverse stories of choice that reflected possibility in their own lives. How might each listener be affected by hearing another person's story? What choice might they conceive which could make a meaningful difference to many? With whom might they share these stories? Where would this information ripple?

What difference can one person make from one choice with one action?

Dr. Rebecca Timlin-Scalera was diagnosed with Stage 4 metastatic breast cancer when she was forty-three, told there was no cure and she had three years to live. A month after her fatal diagnosis, she learned that her cancer was not in her bones, and she was "upgraded" to Stage 3 and could begin to seek a cure.

But what about all the women with Stage 4 cancer she'd met who sat with her in the medical office and hospital waiting rooms? What would happen to them? Could she support them to find a cure versus just extending their lives?

Her choice to not leave these women behind led her to leave her neuropsychology practice and put all her time and energy into her newly created Cancer Couch Foundation, with the mission of raising research funds focused on a cure for metastatic breast cancer.

Rebecca's choice led her to use her medical background to choose the research studies she wanted to fund. She put the fun into her fund-raising efforts and created events that allowed her to invest over three million dollars in research at The Dana Farber Cancer Institute and Memorial Sloan Kettering.

After discovering a video called *The Doorman* about a young man named Josh Yandt who'd been depressed and bullied, I wanted to interview him about the choice he'd made to no longer be invisible upon moving to a new high school. Taking the "small" step to hold the door open was his intention. At first, the kids at his new school looked at him skeptically, unsure of his motives. But then, as they grew comfortable with his actions and greeted his open door with a smile, his simple act of goodwill changed the school's culture.

Pamela Wible, a family practitioner, was disillusioned with the industrialization of the healthcare industry and assembly-line medical care, and chose to create an ideal medical clinic where she could put the patient in charge.

"I'm opening a clinic that'll be designed by you," she told her patients. "Tell me what you want. Tell me your wildest dreams."

And they did—one hundred testimonies worth.

Pamela brought their dreams to life in the first ideal medical clinic in the U.S., where she began providing her patients with a human-scale encounter. Her choice led to a movement where other doctors apply her model to bring ideal medical care to their patients across the country.

My business partner, Eric, and his wife Amy consciously seek opportunities to help others by making an anonymous donation each year. They envision creating a book for their grandchildren that chronicles the stories of their random acts of kindness, hoping their book will be a family legacy allowing future generations to be bitten by the giving bug.

After Eric learned that a single mom, who the family knew distantly, had to spend her scrupulously amassed Christmas savings to replace a totaled car, he and Amy filled an envelope with money. On Christmas morning, a trusted friend knocked on the woman's door, handed her the stuffed envelope, wished her a Merry Christmas and walked away.

Although Eric didn't hear anything more about the donation, he hoped he had given the woman confidence and encouragement during a challenging time.

As I collected and shared these stories, I was struck by the concept that one choice can propagate itself, spreading from one person to the next. Consider the impact Eric's story might have on one person who decides to follow in his footsteps. One seed of one person's idea, which leads to their "small" actions, can make a substantial difference as it ripples beyond them.

From the moment I began paying attention, I heard stories about rippling choices all around me.

After ordering her morning iced coffee in the Starbucks drive-through, a woman chose to pay for the drink ordered by the person in the car behind her. Taking inspiration from the stranger's act of generosity, the second person paid it forward to the third. An unbroken kindness cycle of joy and generosity continued well into the evening. One simple act of generosity connected more than 375 strangers in a beautiful circle of giving.

Our choices can be impactful to others and have reverberations that extend far beyond our visibility. While we may know this to be true, it can feel like a platitude, something disconnected to what we face in daily life.

Your choices can and do lead to ripple effects, whether you're noticing them or not. When you begin to engage with your choices more deeply, you see that they have the ability to create profound momentum and impact, not only in your life but in the lives of others. The ripples stretch beyond what's visible.

PART 6

Taking Maps to the Next Level

Man often becomes what he believes himself to be.
If I keep on saying to myself that I cannot do a certain thing,
it is possible that I may end by really becoming incapable
of doing it. On the contrary, if I have the belief that
I can do it, I shall surely acquire the capacity
to do it even if I may not have it at the beginning.
—Mahatma Gandhi

The power of mapping lies in its versatility and ability to be customized and individualized. There are endless possibilities as to what you can create, and by having a framework of the mapping ingredients, you can adapt and expand upon them to meet your needs.

As you've developed an understanding of how the map elements work, I'd like to share how to take your exploration to the next level, both in how you use the maps and in how you think about the choices you make.

Previously, you've familiarized yourself with the building blocks of mapping:

- Three Choice Mapping™ methods—People Maps, Unfolding Maps and Exploration Maps

- The core Exploration Map questions:

  1. Why does this choice matter to you?

  2. What fears (or limiting beliefs) might get in your way of stepping into the choice?

  3. How do you want to show up as you make your decision?

  4. What may become possible because you make this choice?

  5. What actions will you take to bring your choice to life?

- Suggestions for broader questions depending on the choice you're navigating are gathered on the resource page at http://kimdeyoung.com/ChoiceResources

- How to involve your intuition in the decision-making process

In this section, I'll provide you with examples and stories about enhanced mapping options so you can deepen your inquiry, view your choices from multiple perspectives, and more meaningfully connect with others.

We'll look specifically at:

1. Mapping a choice you've made many times before

2. Repurposing a map of a similar choice

3. Looking at one choice with two map types

4. Finding your way back by being a compassionate listener

CHAPTER 24

Mapping a Choice You've Made Many Times Before

Earlier in the book, I shared a key point that I'd like to reiterate:

What if no choice you made, or could make, was ever wrong?

What if each choice was in your highest good because of the lessons you learned and how it set you up to make better choices going forward?

Whether a particular choice was the best decision of your life or a painful misstep, it added to the lessons of who you are today. In choosing to own where you've been, and by looking at what you did and what you learned, you're able to bring greater consciousness and thoughtfulness to making healthier future choices.

When you approach a situation you've handled before, such as leaving a job or ending a relationship, you may find yourself engulfed in stories or fears of what's happened and how you've handled that choice in the past. By treating your previous choices as valuable lessons that inform your current choices, you can soften your perspective and yield information to best support you moving forward.

To explore a decision you've made before, I'd like to introduce you to using multiple mini-maps. This tool can support you to acknowledge with honesty where you've been and what you've done, and move you into a future that doesn't repeat the same pitfalls or old, unhelpful thinking.

First, let me tell you about a mapping experience I had with a close friend. Then I'll explain how you can apply this approach to your own choice.

During a quiet girl's night, my good friend Becky confided in me about her career pains. Disillusioned by coaching, she considered becoming a writer.

"This is my pattern," she admitted. "I always do this. When things get hard, I leave and look for the next bright shiny object."

"Is that really your truth?" I questioned.

"It feels like it is and I'm worried that I'm going to leave one business for the next and never be satisfied or really accomplish anything."

"Let's look at what actually happened," I suggested.

She agreed and together we created a series of mini Exploration Maps exploring her choice to leave her prior businesses. Each mini-map represented one business.

To see if there were patterns, I asked her a series of questions concerning each of the businesses she had created since her twenties.

- What made you start on that path?
- What did you get out of that business?
- What caused you to move on?
- How did you feel because you moved on?

One by one, as we focused on four past businesses, Becky recalled herself at her younger stages. Taking a closer look at each decision, she noticed behaviors that illustrated her strength, as well as behaviors that showed a tendency to act out of fear. We discovered that she'd begun each business because they all filled a creative need, gave her personal fulfillment and aligned with her values.

When we explored why she'd left each business, she saw a consistent pattern—she left because she wasn't making the money she wanted and, as a result, felt stressed and ashamed. Each time, she felt sad to close the business she loved while also feeling like a failure.

For the existing coaching business she considered leaving, I subtly adjusted the last two questions to the present tense:

- What could cause you to move on?
- How do you feel about moving on?

As she contemplated leaving her current business, she internally berated herself with the question of: Have I failed again?

To dismantle the heaviness and judgment she was feeling, I shifted gears to address her choice to become a writer and began creating a future Exploration Map to infuse this choice with possibility. Through encouraging "what" questions, she was able to view her new choice with curiosity instead of hesitation and see the field of possibilities laid out before her.

- What makes writing a book an important next step for you?
- What would make writing fun?
- What would keep you engaged in the process?
- What might cause you to walk away?
- What makes writing the book a success?

In the wake of our conversation, Becky settled into a place of self-acceptance and appreciation. She discovered that writing a book would be healing and allow her to integrate the many aspects of her extraordinary background into one offering. Realizing that a book would provide a solid foundation from which to offer other services, she began to feel hopeful and excited. Reexamining one choice she made repeatedly allowed her to process her remorse and view the past with empathy, enabling her to move forward.

Let me share how you can apply the concept of mini-mapping to a choice you've made numerous times before. As an example, we'll use the choice to end past relationships.

Take yourself back in time and truly consider who you were at the juncture of each relationship-ending decision—what you were feeling, and what you were experiencing. Create a mini-map of each relationship using these nonjudgmental and less emotionally-charged questions.

- What motivated you to start this relationship? (Imagine yourself in the early stages of that relationship envisioning what you hoped for.)
- What did you learn from it? (Go as deep as you'd like with this one: consider the good and the bad, what you experienced and how you grew.)

- What prompted you to move on? (Was this decision made on your own or with support? Had you been considering it for a while? Was there a final-straw circumstance?)

- What were your feelings after you moved on? (Sad, remorseful, unrestrained, courageous…)

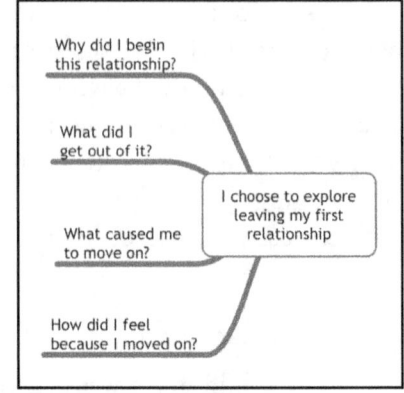

If you're considering leaving your current relationship, you can adapt the final two mini-map questions to the present tense:

- What could cause you to move on?

- What is your feeling about moving on?

Asking "what" questions naturally evokes curiosity, leading to more open-hearted responses. Should you feel judgment toward your younger self for how you felt or what you did, observe yourself with the compassion you'd wish to impart to a friend or child. Remember that you did your best with the circumstances you were in at the time.

After completing each mini-map, place them side-by-side on one page, scanning for patterns amidst your answers. When you examine several examples of one choice concurrently, you may be able to identify common threads and new realizations that will inform your next decision.

To see what this looks like in action, here's a template of a mini-map and the completed series of maps.

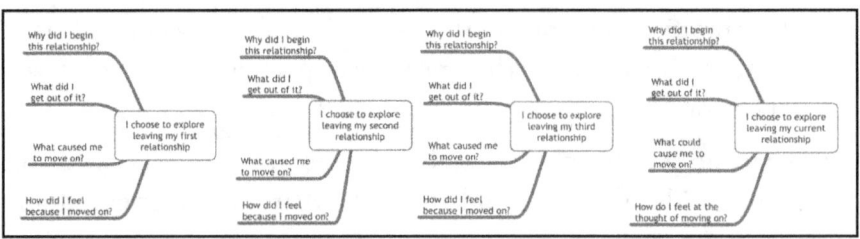

In the final step, using the insights gleaned from looking back, you'll create a future Exploration Map for the new relationship you hope to enter.

- What makes you want to enter this relationship?
- What would make this relationship fun?
- What would keep you engaged with this person?
- What might cause you to walk away?
- What would make this relationship a success?

Comparing mini-maps side-by-side facilitates witnessing the truth of your stories clearly, allowing you to extract insights from previous experiences that you can apply to future choices. Instead of facing a problem to be overcome, or a personal defect that needs to be fixed, you can view your history with fresh eyes and sympathetic consideration. Using the knowledge gained from your past review as a foundation for your future map, you can anticipate what's possible with enthusiasm. Using this tool, you can objectively acknowledge your past actions and prevent yourself from repeating familiar, default responses as you step into the future. The concept of examining multiple choices together can be applied to your personal choices as well as guiding a friend through an exploration of theirs.

CHAPTER 25

Repurposing a Map

In the previous chapter, we looked at how mapping a choice you've made many times can help you visualize patterns, gain new insights and use the information you garnered to inform your next decision. In this chapter, we'll continue to look at choices you've made in the past, but from the vantage point of repurposing past maps as you prepare to make a similar choice. As an alternative to starting from scratch, using a completed map as a skeleton simplifies the process of exploring a current choice.

The beauty of initially investing time to create a well-crafted Exploration Map is that the concepts are evergreen. A map that embodies all you want, all you're scared of, all that's possible and the actions you'll take will be applicable to a future version of the same choice. A majority of your answers will be similar, and will provide a template for generating new information.

In my map-making journey, I've created many maps with clients related to the following choices:

- Choosing to work with a new business partner
- Choosing to date a new man

First, I'll share an example of how a client repurposed her past maps regarding working with a new business partner. Then, I'll explain how you can apply this simple technique to your specific choice.

A few years ago, Traci, a business consultant, landed a highly coveted opportunity to help a dream client significantly grow her company. To envision undertaking this project and the expansiveness of its possibilities, she created her first Exploration Map stating: *I choose to fully embrace the opportunity of working with my ideal client.*

Using her values as a guide, she customized the questions on her map:

- What makes this position exciting and fun?
- How would stepping into this role enrich me personally and professionally?
- In order for me to thrive and grow, what would make our working relationship ideal?
- What fears and limiting beliefs need to be acknowledged and released?
- How will I commit to showing up?
- By collaborating, what will become possible for each of us individually and collectively?
- In regard to my existing clients, what actions will I take?

It took several hours to craft her map, fine-tuning the words until they echoed her clear message. The branches groaned with mentions of her biggest fear—being dependent on one client. She'd deliberately kept her clientele small and diversified, and the thought of walking away from them for the opportunity of a new prospect terrified her most.

What if it didn't work? What would she fall back on?

Her map also chronicled her aspirations. While dreaming what was possible with this new partner, Traci identified with her desire to work on meaningful, fulfilling projects that would more fully utilize her talents. Her map grew to extend beyond this one opportunity, encompassing a broader range of possibilities for her professional life.

When she contrasted her fears with the potential of working with a smart, talented team, she felt thrilled. Having the chance to enhance her skills, make new connections and be compensated for her efforts in the company's growth were exciting opportunities.

As Traci contemplated the polarity between her fears and potential-filled future, she felt optimistic about what could be. Unfortunately, weeks passed without the anticipated offer, and the partnership never materialized.

Initially, she felt despondent for dreaming, discouraged that the time and effort she'd put into creating her map had been in vain.

"There will be new prospects coming your way," I confidently predicted, "and the time you've spent creating your map, and thinking about what's possible, can be repurposed for a different opportunity."

As one of my first clients to understand the value of mapping, Traci began to use the information gathered in her well-crafted maps to guide her important professional decisions. Now, when she stands at the crossroads of working with a new client, she repurposes a previous Exploration Map to assess if the prospective client is the right fit. She duplicates her original map and refreshes the details. Since the questions to consider and many of her answers are consistent, she updates the map with specifics about who the client is and what their needs are.

Returning to an older version of a map and using it as a base allows you to reinvigorate it with the details of your current scenario.

A map, lovingly attended to, is a repository for all that's possible, ready to be unsealed and drawn upon when it may be difficult to recount.

Consider that you've previously created a well-thought out map about the decision: *I choose to take a new job.*

Likely, you'll make that choice again, and when you do, you'll have a base of questions and answers to work from, to freshen up. You'll simply duplicate your original map, and update it with the specifics of your current job opportunity.

CHAPTER 26

Looking at One Choice Through Two Maps

Throughout this book, you've learned how to approach choice through making a map:

- An Unfolding Map allows you to look at how a choice progresses chronologically and what it brings into your life.

- An Exploration Map is guided by inquiry and distills the complexities of a choice into simpler, clearer nuggets.

As you explore a choice you made or one you are making, you may find it beneficial and enlightening to look at one choice through the lens of both an Exploration Map and an Unfolding Map to provide you with additional insights.

This two-map approach naturally lends itself to deep-diving into one of your *five intentional choices* that led you to where you are today (see Chapter 2 for a refresher). I've used one of my five choices as an example. It can also be used for any past choice that feels significant and that had a great impact on you.

Let me explain how to get started and then I'll share a personal example so that you can see these steps in action. Essentially, you're going to create an Exploration Map for your choice, and then an Unfolding Map for the same choice.

Here's a review of how to create these maps.

1. First you'll create a **past Exploration Map** for a significant past choice with the following questions:

   - What led you to make this choice?

   - What fears did you have to overcome that could have prevented you from making this choice?

   - What limiting beliefs did you need to reframe so you could move forward?

   - How did you show up at that time?

   - What did you think might happen?

   - How did this choice affect your life?

2. If you want to dig deeper, you'll ask additional "what" questions that will support you to unearth more information. (See the resource page at http://kimdeyoung.com/ChoiceResources for an in-depth list of questions related to what you hoped for, how you made your choice, what its impact was and what you learned.)

3. Once you've created your past Exploration Map, you'll turn your attention to chronology instead of exploration to develop a past Unfolding Map related to the same choice.

   - For your Unfolding Map, you'll note your choice on the left.

   - On the right, you'll sequentially plot the opportunities, experiences, thoughts and people who came into your life from that choice.

   - You'll distinguish what happened because of your deliberate actions, and what appeared due to synchronicities outside your control.

   - Should you be exploring a choice made decades ago, consider sticking to key milestones in your Unfolding Map versus capturing every detail.

Earlier in the book, I described creating an Exploration Map called *Art History as a Turning Point*. The goal was to understand my twenty-year-old self's motivations, fears, limiting beliefs and dreams when I broadened my college major to include Art History. After engaging with the Exploration Map's questions, I observed that a "simple" choice made in my twenties had ramifications that impacted my life well into my fifties.

My Exploration Map began with: *I chose to add art history to my college major.* In considering how this youthful decision affected my life, I acknowledged that it was the gateway to confronting the limiting belief that had held me back for decades: *I'm not creative.*

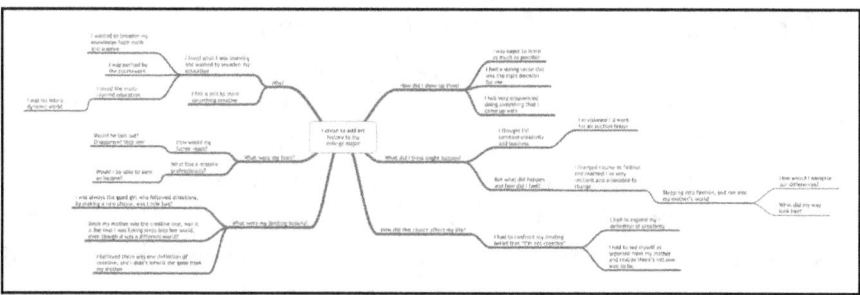

With the intention of moving beyond this belief, I sought the assistance of a beloved coach who helped me broaden my definition of creativity, which originally maintained that one must be neat and paint within the lines.

Appreciating that there was still more to comprehend about the opportunities I had, what occurred and the path I forged, I created a corresponding Unfolding Map, which enabled me to visualize my choice from another perspective, yielding different results and insights.

I sequentially documented *My Creative Journey* in an Unfolding Map to look at how my college decision and its aftereffects had an impact on the navigation of my life. Visually, I could see how my decision to study Art History extended into future decades, a thread that wove its way through my life and professional experiences. With the Unfolding Map, I could connect dots and observe how a "small" choice made at twenty paved the way to my corporate career in the fashion industry, led to my future decision to step into the entrepreneurial world and ultimately showed up in my decision to divorce.

The Exploration Map documented what I learned and how I grew. Then, the Unfolding Map sequentially chronicled the tracking of my life. Since my Unfolding Map covered such a broad time frame, it was more important to capture major milestones rather than to record every person, experience and opportunity I encountered.

Observing all that had unfolded, I visually noted the stepping stones that appeared one by one, guiding me in an unanticipated and productive direction. My Unfolding Map made it clear that studying Art History was my first step toward my own version of creativity, which was the common thread that emerged in the jobs I chose, how I began to see myself, the gifts I stepped into and the future opportunities that awaited me. Seeing my life as a creative journey honors and highlights the thread of my connection to my mother, whose creativity I aspired to emulate throughout my childhood.

Approaching the same choice through two perspectives—one detailed and one chronological—demonstrates the significance that one choice can have across the breadth of your life, instilling a reverence for decisions you've made that remain a piece of you today.

The choices you've made are woven into who you are. In pulling at these threads, you access your past and future selves, bringing together what you've learned with what you're seeking.

Looking at all you've done, it's easier to imagine all that lies ahead.

CHAPTER 27

Finding Your Way Back by Being a Compassionate Listener

In previous chapters, maps have had an internal focus—concentrated solely on reviewing and exploring your choices. In this chapter, I'll guide you in applying the mapping concepts externally to strengthen your connection with others.

One of the benefits to becoming more proficient at mapping is that you're simultaneously becoming more proficient at asking thought-provoking questions, drawing out additional information and listening more attentively—skills that serve you both in the context of mapping as well as in the context of being an open-hearted, compassionate listener.

Whether you're helping a friend, colleague or family member work through a map of their own, or simply navigating a relationship, mapping provides a means of approaching conversations about other people's choices from the stance of the observer, acting as a sympathetic gatherer of information. As you compile content for their map, the pace of your conversation naturally relaxes, enabling you to be fully present. In seeking to connect more deeply with another and give them the gift of feeling heard, you're listening intently for their unplanned responses without seeking to solve their problems. You're capturing ideas and making connections, noticing where there's more substance to unearth. By extracting their buried thoughts, you're assisting them to make sense of a time that warrants attention.

The act of entering into a sacred space to explore another person's choice, and perhaps even their heart, gives you the opportunity to reach a deeper level of connection and intimacy.

Let me take you inside two personal experiences where I discovered the potency of this practice first hand.

In the introduction to my book, I reveal that years ago I made a life-defining choice to end my contentious relationship with my mother. Shortly after making that decision, I became engrossed in the adventure of mapping.

My mother was not aware of my journey.

The day I welcomed her back into my life and subsequently into my journey with maps was the day my life and my heart opened.

It started when, prompted by my coach, I connected with my father in order to learn more about my grandmother, a woman I never knew. Through that interaction with my father, my toughened exterior softened and I felt an emotional stirring to reconnect with my mother. After having barely spoken with her for two years, I courageously asked if she'd like to get together.

Without hesitation she said yes and I initiated our first private conversation in what felt like an eternity. While sitting in our favorite coffee shop, I began to "date" my mother, getting to know her again, tentatively.

As we slowly danced amidst our emotional debris, I kept a guarded wall around my maps—never envisioning telling her about them, and certainly never intending to do one for her.

Then, one afternoon a month or so later, in a tender moment, I invited her into my world and asked if she'd like to see what I was working on.

To my surprise and delight she said yes.

Sitting side-by-side in front of my computer, I shared the visuals of dozens of maps, explaining the stories of people whose choices I'd explored. As her eyes moved across the screen taking in details, she was captivated, eager to know more about each person's story.

"Kim, I'm beyond intrigued. This is the most incredible thing I've ever seen you do."

"Thank you."

And in words that surprised me as they passed my lips, I offered, "Would you like me to do one for you?"

"Yes!" she answered eagerly, without a trace of reluctance. "What would I need to do?"

"Think of a choice you'd like to explore and we'll go from there."

"Do I need to prepare other than having my choice?" she questioned.

"Not at all. That's the beauty of the process. We'll spend time together and I'll let my curious mind run wild by asking questions about your choice and allowing our conversation to roam. I'll take notes and you can enjoy the experience of focusing on what you recall."

During our exploration, we delved into my mother's choice more than fifty years earlier not to take a language in school. When a conscientious guidance counselor noticed the vacancy in her ninth-grade schedule, she presented my mother with the possibility of taking fashion classes for the balance of high school and then attending the Fashion Institute of Technology for her college experience.

As my mother described the unexpected turns this shift into fashion created, my inquisitive nature provided the backdrop for her stories to flow. Some stories I knew, many I didn't. For years I'd been guarded in our interactions, but as we consciously stepped into the exploration process, I allowed myself to be curious, engaging her with questions that let us peek beneath the surface and create connections between threads of her life.

I took her on a journey—a journey we both needed more than we realized. I questioned. I listened. I heard. Making sense of her stories gave me a deeper appreciation for a woman I'd become increasingly distant from.

My childhood home was an homage to my mother's creative prowess, featuring elaborate geometric designs. Although I was fascinated with her perfection, I felt an inner sadness that I was not like her. Where her creativity was rooted in precision and order, mine was out-of-the-box, more messy, less linear. She sews beautifully, taking time to do the pre-work before her sewing begins. By contrast, I staple the hem of my pants. I bought into the limiting belief that her way was the only way to be creative, and I didn't inherit that gene.

Wanting to understand how she'd become the artist she is, I posed questions about her practice. I discovered that her passion for painting with geometric perfection stemmed from her youthful love of design, numbers and spatial relations. She was enthralled with the precision of plaids.

In the simplicity of the small but powerful five-letter word *plaid*, I saw our differences clearly, in a way I never had. Plaid symbolized her regimentation, her quest for order, a word that had no relation to who I was. Witnessing the structured plaid as a metaphor for our disparity, I understood that neither of us was right or wrong, we were simply different. After finding peace with our differences, feelings of inadequacy and judgment that I'd carried for years no longer needed to be part of the story I perpetuated about my mother.

For ten hours, over three days, I listened with an open heart. Giving her space to share a lifetime of stories, I found myself loving her for all she was and forgiving her for all she was not. I appreciated being in the role of asking her questions and letting her shine, a place she's rarely had the opportunity to stand. In a particularly touching moment, after much time immersed in the intricacies of her life, I told my mother I loved her, words I'd not articulated in over thirty years.

The mapping and inquiry process allowed my mother and I to reconnect at a deep and poignant level, and I found myself viewing her through a much kinder and more empathetic lens. After our in-depth time together she shared, "I find your process to be more valuable than years of therapy because you've listened so intentionally and we've covered so much of my life in such a short period of time. You've helped me to make connections between parts of my life that I hadn't seen before. It's a fascinating perspective."

We wrapped up my mom's map as I was about to turn fifty. Having no plans for my birthday, she asked if I'd like to travel with her and my father for a few days. Years, or even months before, that conversation would have been a fantasy. But on that day, her question, and my ultimate response of yes, was as natural as if there had never been any pain between us.

A few years later, as we coped with my father's rapid degeneration from Alzheimer's, we were connected, aligned and able to care for him together without the added burden of our previous detachment. On his seventy-eighth birthday, a birthday he did not recognize, my mom and I discussed that the time had come to move him to a memory care facility. As I shared how much I loved her and wanted to stand by her during this awful time, I reminded her how fortunate we are that we found our way back to each other.

"Imagine the discomfort of caring for dad if we'd been burdened with our past rift and disdain," I observed.

The process of exploring her choice and giving her a chance to share openly provided us with a safe and neutral space to find our way back to the relationship that mattered to us. Had it not been for the experience of creating her map, which involved listening with openness and compassion, she and I would not have healed years of pain, judgment and disconnect.

While I enjoy mapping immensely, as is evident, I also truly appreciate what mapping affords you the ability to do. As you connect with someone you care for and bring your enhanced map-thinking skills of listening coupled with your sensitivity to asking thoughtful questions, you demonstrate reverence for the other person's situation.

Reaching the tender spot in another person's heart begins with a meaningful conversation. The more adept you become at asking good questions, the more compassionately you can engage with the people who matter to you, even those with whom you're having challenging dynamics.

When you feel isolated from a relationship, whether it's with a romantic partner, parent, child, friend, sibling or even a business partner, you can use Choice Mapping to engage in a dialogue that will allow you to connect more deeply and address unresolved resentments and feelings about past interactions or experiences that have likely gone unspoken.

Mapping provides a resource to engage in a conversation to heal your rift, to support you to identify the root cause of your disconnect. It's a tool to enable you to listen without judgment and speak without anger. When you've lost your way, mapping supports you to find your way back.

Building on the mapping experience I had with my mother, I want to share a healing encounter I had with my daughter to exemplify how beneficial it can be to use mapping to connect with someone you care for. I'll first take you behind the scenes to explain what happened with her, and then I'll share how you can apply this questioning to yourself and a loved one.

During my daughter Tasha's first semester of her sophomore year in college we went through a challenge in our personal connection. She wanted a level of independence that was normal for a nineteen-year-old, and I was finding my way with how to give it to her while also wanting to stay involved as her parent. It seemed that no matter what I did or said we clashed, and our communication was stilted and tenuous. I often felt her eye-rolling through the Wi-Fi of our phones.

When she returned home for her winter break, we talked about the pain of our estrangement. I suggested we create a map to unearth the issues that had caused our separation with the goal of finding our way back to each other.

"I'd love that," she said, "I've missed you. How should we begin?"

"Let's start with you describing what happened for you."

As we sat in the quiet of the kitchen and she recounted details of what caused her to pull away from me, I captured her words in branches of a new Exploration Map that began with our collective choice: *We choose to find our way back to each other.*

She described how she'd changed a lot during sophomore year and had begun making decisions on her own. She explained how she'd developed a deeper understanding of her pain from our divorce and that she was making sense of how it affected her behaviors. The specific details she expressed were uncomfortable to hear. I refrained from getting defensive, kept listening and continued asking probing questions to better comprehend the nuances of her experience.

Capturing her words in a map allowed me to clearly see the parts of our conversation that required expansion. I noticed where I needed to ask more questions to fill in blank spaces and where to just listen. No judgment.

After an hour of what felt like an incredibly deep therapy session, listening to her speak with great candor and incredible wisdom, we took a break.

The following day I noticed that the heavy energy which had existed between us for months had dissipated and there was a playfulness in our communication.

"Do you feel a shift in us today?" I wondered out loud.

"Yes, it feels so much easier to be with you," she admitted.

"What do you think caused this?" I inquired curiously.

With great insight, she said, "You listened to me without judgment and didn't try to fix me, and that felt really good."

Listen without judgment. So simple, so textbook, yet so hard to actually do and such an incredible gift to both of us when done. Giving her the space to share her fears and upsets, no matter how dark, without providing my typical parental solution for how to make them go away, was what she needed. In the past, because of my desire to ease her pain and fix her problems, I was inadvertently hindering her ability to find her way and develop her own process.

Should your interactions with someone you care about feel tentative and strained let me suggest how to begin a dialogue with them.

"I've missed you." You tell them.

"Can we talk?" You invite them.

You present a loving offering, not knowing what lies beyond that cracked-open door.

As you vulnerably share that you miss them and long for connection:

- You let them know things are tense and you're willing to accept responsibility for your part.

- To reconnect, you want to hear about their experience and how they feel in order to uncover unspoken words that may help to resolve your issues.

- You want to understand whether your actions are causing them pain.

- You crave being honest and open so you can address any pebbles or rocks before they become boulders.

To begin, you must have buy-in from both sides, with each of you willing to show up committed, open and ready to let go of defensiveness. Neither is being dragged into the experience by the other.

For you, as the facilitator and keeper of the map, your role is to create a sacred space for this conversation with a clear time boundary, ideally no more than an hour. This work is deep and emotional and once your truths are shared, your words need time to marinate, to seep into each of your thoughts.

To avoid bringing an agenda to the experience, you show up without an expectation of fixing anything, being right or hashing out an issue. Instead, you show up to hold space and engage in a heartfelt dialogue.

Your collective choice is: *We choose to find our way back to each other.*

The process begins by guiding them with one question: What caused you to lose your way?

The dialogue is then fueled by the power of continued inquiry, diving deeper with each question, trusting that when they provide an answer, you'll take it in without defensiveness and guide them to the next question. Through your questions, the dialogue that ensues allows them to feel heard and understood.

The benefit of using the map is it keeps you focused on one question, one answer. Your focus is solely on asking—not solving or fixing. You're using the map to capture answers to questions for which you're being the observer, listening with compassion and empathy. The healthy distance created by your inquiry keeps any temptation to jump in with a quick answer or an obvious fix.

Creating a map as you communicate makes your role clear—you're thoughtfully gleaning and organizing information, showing an interest in what's being expressed, rather than weighing in.

Listening and capturing their answers lets you visually see where there's more to draw out. Should you witness underdeveloped branches of their map, asking questions with focused curiosity will flesh out additional narrative.

One of the strengths of mapping lies in slowing down the thought processes that typically cause us to race to conclusions, ignoring or overlooking important nuances and details that can shed light on the motives and mechanics underlying our choices.

Final Nuggets
Mapping Without a Map

Look at the journey you've taken. Look at the courage you've embodied and the vulnerability you've shown in exploring your past, your present and your future. Look at the clarity you've been able to distill from previously unfamiliar and complex concepts.

Take a moment to appreciate what you've discovered—a new lens through which to examine the choices you make every day while bringing a sacred quality to the experience.

This is exquisite.

An unexpected aspect of this journey is your ability to transcend the map—to map without needing a physical map.

This may seem like an unusual way to end the book after devoting twenty-seven chapters to describing how to create a wide variety of maps. While I absolutely love maps and everything about the process of mapping, the most priceless gifts you've given yourself by taking the concepts of this book to heart are your abilities to:

- ask inspiring and thought-provoking questions
- listen intently with compassion and without judgment (both to yourself and others)
- create space for contemplation and unfolding to occur

As you navigate your life, making choices and engaging in meaningful conversations, you won't always have your computer, a piece of paper or a desire to write. What you will always have is the ability to ask insightful questions.

Mapping includes the tangible component of a physical map, but perhaps more importantly, it encompasses the intangible, internal dimension of processing information mindfully.

Whether you create a visual map of the questions and answers related to your choice, or think through them without a map, you're drawing upon the skills you've developed in the book's chapters.

Living an examined life is a practice. Mapping can support you to heal yourself, to connect with others more deeply, and to look at your life, what was and what may be, with incredible consciousness. Life is an ever-evolving journey that calls for consistent self-reflection and self-awareness.

May this book and the tools within be a resource for you to return to at key junctures. May this book be a treasure you share with your friends, family and children as they seek to bring a greater level of thought and consciousness to their choices. May you find yourself becoming, more and more, an intrepid explorer of life, your choices a map leading back home to your own heart.

Acknowledgements

It takes a village.

Over a nine-year window, I built and rebuilt this book five times. I've overhauled the structure, tossed sections, added and deleted maps, and reorganized stories to best share my message. With the support of encouraging coaches and editors, I recognized when I was succumbing to the illusion that I'd written my best words in a prior iteration and had no more to give. Envisioning you, my reader, benefitting immensely from these concepts and this conversation, I persevered, knowing it was my mission to bring you the message that has been gifted to me.

Had I begun writing this book the day the idea downloaded into my thoughts, it wouldn't be what it has ultimately become. The initial idea required time to germinate. I've woken up to record messages from dreams. I've paused movies to capture sentences that deserved further development. I've transcribed conversations that held important insights.

The message of choice lives in and around me, beckoning me to pay attention. Allowing myself time and space encouraged me to create a richer work than if I'd bowed to the pressure to begin immediately.

Gratitude for the Maps

I feel immense gratitude for the gift of the maps, for the journey they've taken me on, and for the deep connection with others they've facilitated.

I'm often asked how I found the maps; in reality, the maps found me. Their evolution unfolded in a stunning manner. I wasn't seeking them, never envisioned them and most certainly did not have a plan for what they'd ultimately become.

I feel gratitude that many of the maps I created for others were mirrors of my own life, containing messages and nuggets that were important for me to hear and internalize personally.

- Do not give your power to the guru.
- You have the answers within you.
- There is great power in forgiveness.
- From one choice, one book, one person, an entire world can open up.

Had it not been for the experience of mapping, I would not have found my way back to my mother. For that I am most grateful.

The Initial Mapping Journey

My initial thanks goes to the special people in my life who allowed the mapping journey to begin. My acknowledgements read much like a People Map—so much has bloomed from the seed of connections I formed with a few key people.

Fabienne Fredrickson hosted the workshop that sparked my first map, which I shared in the introduction. She was the coach who supported me as I began my entrepreneurial journey. Had I not accepted her event's invitation, this book would not exist.

Donna Cravotta consoled me after having made the life-defining choice to end my relationship with my mother. Donna's belief in me at a time when I was desolate allowed my first Unfolding Map to grow. She has been my angel, cheering me on for more than a decade.

Nancy Marmolejo is my dear friend who, after sharing my first map, asked me to do one for her. I said yes and plunged into the experience not knowing where it was going. Nancy is also the key person who urged me to enjoy the mapping experience without needing to know what would emerge. Without heeding Nancy's advice, the maps and their process might not exist today. Her words allowed me to deeply dive into an opportunity, ripe with potential.

Melanie Benson asked me a question during an interview a decade ago that sparked a divine download of an idea that developed into this book. In an uncanny coincidence, she was also connected to the first person who encouraged me to write a book.

When I read Bob Burg's *The Go-Giver* years ago, his message about being of service had a profound effect on me, and I interviewed him in 2010. During our discussion, he shared that he believed I had a book inside of me, and was excited to read it when it ultimately came out. This touched me greatly. While I knew there was a truth in his words, in 2010 I had no vision for what the book might be.

After Melanie's interview, when the book idea came to me, I was excited to share with Bob that I'd finally found inspiration for the book he predicted. As I shared how the idea came about in my conversation with Melanie, he was amused to tell me that he and Melanie not only knew each other, but had spoken the day before. Watching these seemingly separate pieces come together, it's easy to understand how I was inspired to map out these "coincidences" and track their path through my life. I'm grateful to Bob for implanting the initial seed of belief that a book lay within me.

The Mappies

My next heartfelt thanks extends to the initial twenty-nine fascinating people who said yes to participating in a mapping experience. It is through their stories that this book has come to life.

None knew what the process entailed, but they eagerly said yes to my question: *would you like to explore a choice?* Each person answered the intuitive questions that channeled through me with grace and without resistance. I'm honored they felt safe embarking upon an unknown journey with me, jumping in with vulnerability and enthusiasm, sharing experiences, feelings and thoughts which may never have been voiced before.

In the early months, new to the mapping experience, I did not physically create the maps while engaged in a deep dive conversation. It took time to develop the capacity to ask questions and map concurrently. Instead, I took copious notes, listening for nuggets of wisdom and truth. Hours later, after their words marinated in my thoughts, I retreated into my creative cave with my mind-mapping software to make sense of what was shared.

I'd unweave their story, taking a first pass at creating branches, moving words around, and coming back two, three and four times to finesse them. The process of translating their words and message into this structure revealed meaning that had been obscured—thoughts that might have felt ordinary announced their greater importance. It took significant trust, which I didn't always have, that their words would guide me.

The process I've shared throughout the book's chapters evolved slowly over many maps through practice. Each map took hours to craft—hours that were joyous as I imagined how I'd present their words back to them, providing a new perspective through which to view their choice.

I changed the names and identifying details of each "mappy" for their privacy. They've been assigned pseudonyms that belong to others who are dear to me. Through this rechristening, I am able to bring the presence of even more of my most special people into this book.

My Coaches & Editors

Having the inspiration and the idea for a book was one thing—writing it was entirely another. I feel deep gratitude for the coaches and editors who supported me in the creation of *The Book of Choice*. Each saw greater potential in what I could do than I saw for myself, and each held space for me to step into what I wanted, even when I wasn't sure how I would get there.

A year into my mapping journey, I decided it was time to start writing my book rather than just dreaming about it. Not believing I was a writer, I hired Kate Brenton, the most perfect coach for me at that time. Without knowing what our process would be, I freely jumped into my writing journey, trusting she'd guide me along the way.

I made it clear to Kate that I was not a writer. "I'll be the judge of that," she staunchly declared.

Kate provided me with short writing prompts and instructed me to write for no more than twelve minutes. Each Monday through Thursday morning, in my quaint local coffee shop with a frothy cappuccino and my favorite music, I committed to writing before I did anything else. With my earbuds in place, I'd shut out the world and type for twelve minutes. Through Kate's prompts, I developed a rhythm of writing and letting my thoughts flow without purpose, without a destination and without judgment. I didn't worry about what I was writing—I simply answered her queries, followed interesting tangents and shared my stories.

For weeks I enthusiastically woke up early to head to the creative haven of my coffee shop. Typing for short sprints built my writing muscle, and gave me confidence that a writer existed within me.

After a month of working with Kate, she suggested I begin crafting my words with the book's message in mind. Using the maps as my springboard, my writing flowed and it was a glorious process to construct dialogue from the maps' branches. Although the writing came easily, I expressed my concern to Kate.

"I think I'm cheating," I shared. "I'm taking the conversations and experiences directly from the maps."

"Why do you think you're cheating? You created the maps," she said, pointing out what should have been obvious.

Kate suggested I reframe my thinking. "Can you acknowledge that you spent your time having a deep intake with another person about their choice, and from that intake you used your intuitive process to create your maps, and from those maps the dialogue emerged?"

Rather than make myself small by calling myself a cheater, I owned that I had an unusual process. Due to my deep mapping conversations capturing large amounts of information, I found it fun to narrate the map details in story form.

"Your words are liquid gold," Kate said. "I want more of these stories. Keep capturing them."

And so I did.

Jen Odear was my business copywriter prior to the book's idea emerging. She supported me to get my voice onto paper, knowing I dreaded the blank page. She would craft my bullet-pointed ideas into close-to-perfect paragraphs that I'd tweak to reflect my unique voice. We had a beautiful back-and-forth writing dynamic. Jen understood both me and my vision, and stood beside me for years helping me make sense of the value of mapping. Jen's advice and insights were instrumental in the early iterations of the book.

Two years into my writing journey, Elise Panza Borbely entered my world.

Elise is my naturopathic physician, intuitive healer and medical detective. As we each grew intrigued with the other, I did a map for her about a professional choice she was navigating. I shared initial chapters of an early iteration of the book and she provided exceptionally insightful and thoughtful feedback.

In my usual intuitively guided way, without knowing if Elise had writing experience, I invited her to become my editor. I learned after the fact that she had a degree from Yale and had worked in developmental editing. I hired her for her heart and her passion, not realizing she had the writing expertise that would become an unbelievable gift in what this book has become.

In previous versions of the book, though it's hard to believe now, the maps were essentially a footnote. As we structured and restructured the book, refining concepts to their essence, Elise made the revolutionary suggestion that I create a chapter explaining how to make a map.

This was not on my radar prior to Elise's invitation. The idea of teaching or sharing maps never crossed my mind—they were my private process done behind the scenes to provide people with value and a new perspective. Never did I envision anyone wanting to see my method and adopt it for themselves.

Intrigued with her idea, I created a map called *How to Make a Map*. As I sat perched on my own shoulder, I observed how I'd been doing what I'd been doing, a process I'd never articulated.

In this map, I clarified the definitions of People, Unfolding and Exploration Maps. I determined we make past, present and future choices which fall into personal, professional and relationship choice buckets. I thought through the questions I asked for each type of choice.

Once I defined the mapping process, and Elise began to experiment with it herself, I realized there was something interesting at play that I must add to the book.

Acknowledgements

Early in my writing journey I was connected to Kelly Notaras, writer, editor and founder of kn literary. I followed her work attentively, reading and listening to her every word as if she were speaking directly to me.

Pre-pandemic and on the book's third iteration, I scheduled a coaching call with Kelly to help me to navigate the complexity that the book had become part memoir, part process and part love story.

"It can't be all three," she vehemently said. "I recommend that as a first time author you focus on the process. Your memoir can come later."

Appreciating her suggestion, I diligently got to work highlighting, editing and keeping stories that supported the mapping process, and removing personal stories that did not. I rearranged the book substantially.

Three weeks after meeting Kelly, my dad died quite suddenly and I put the book away, again.

Many months later, when I had energy and a desire to skim through the manuscript, the fourth iteration took me by surprise. In my grief, I had lost touch with the content, and this new version, stripped of many of my stories to focus more pointedly on choice and maps, felt disorienting. I was overwhelmed.

I'd begun coaching with Steph Jagger, a twice published author, because I was drawn to her books, her story and her writing style. During one of our coaching calls, which had nothing to do with writing, Steph said, "Would it be helpful to you if I reviewed your manuscript?"

"Yes," I eagerly replied.

While preparing to send Steph my manuscript, I felt deep anxiety and shared, "I think I need to redo the book and remove everything related to the maps. The whole thing feels overly complicated. The book should only be about choice, and not include anything about mapping."

"On a scale of 1 to 10, how true is that statement?" Steph questioned.

"An 11," I stated with absolute conviction.

"Kim, send me the book. Let me review it and then we'll have a conversation."

After she'd thoroughly read it she said, "The maps must stay, they're your differentiating factor. However, right now, the way the book is written, it's too complicated. You're opening the book with your most complex maps. You're asking your reader to jump into the deep end before they've had a chance to wade into the shallow waters.

"Your book needs to be pulled apart and simplified. You must bring your reader with you on a journey. You must give them a vocabulary and an understanding of your tools so that they can digest the concepts. As they get comfortable with your ideas, you can take them deeper, ultimately sharing your more detailed concepts."

Her words were irrefutable but challenging to take in as it meant returning to my pages for a full revamp.

So began iteration five.

How would I make what was complex simple? I asked myself.

I rearranged the book per Steph's suggested structure, moved my most complex maps to the final chapters, and rewrote the early chapters to provide you with a vocabulary, lexicon and simple mapping templates. With a strong foundation, it now feels exciting to invite you into the more intricate sections later in the book.

As Steph's words—*Wade them in slowly*—continued to ring in my thoughts, Elise was by my side, whether physically co-writing from a local coffee shop (a favorite time for me), or at a distance collaborating in a Google doc. She embraced Kelly's and Steph's words. She heard them all plus she knew my heart and mission. She's known every iteration, and held me while I wrote, revised, edited and tweaked. She's helped to massage my thoughts and find the words when I felt stuck. And always, she brought her magic.

Claire Gerdes joined me at the end of the writing and editing process to bring her proofreading prowess. Claire offers a special touch that is uniquely hers—she has the gift of grammar, word choice, fluidity, consistency and clarity. Claire reads with the goal of making sense of the nuts and bolts of the details. For her kindness and attention to every minute detail, I am so grateful. Claire also gathered valuable nuggets of content from the manuscript for me to share with new followers.

The Beta Readers

Thank you to the handful of friends, aka beta readers, who offered to read the book after I'd completed my final edits. I took their comments to heart and feel deep appreciation that they each invested their time and insights to support me to bring this book to you. Thank you especially to Jenny Vannier who had the courage to share difficult-to-hear feedback that caused me to drastically improve the introduction.

My Creative Support

I want to share my appreciation for Heather Neilson. When I first began writing, I tracked many ideas of where the maps might lead—one was a dream of creating maps three dimensionally. While visiting a loft space filled with many artists, I found myself drawn to Heather's studio. With art, paint and creativity everywhere in the room, I sensed she was meant to be my next guide.

Feeling pandemic stagnancy in my writing, I registered for Heather's painting class, hoping to infuse my energy with creativity. Every week, armed with my tote bag of new art supplies, I drove two hours to paint in Heather's studio. She guided me to paint intuitively, to put marks on the canvas and respond to them with elements that called to me, to let my painting be a call-and-response experience. The lessons in the art studio translated to my writing. As I began to work on the fifth iteration, I wrote before I painted and painted before I wrote.

I worked with Michelle Radomski twice on the book's cover design. First, when the book's name was *The Alchemy of Choice*, and then for its current title. The experience of working with her is intuitive and expansive. It's a joy to experience her creative flow. I specifically hired

Michelle for her artistic background because I knew she'd present the maps in a manner that's visually accessible.

My Loved Ones

I want to thank my special friends who were a part of my journey from the beginning—Laura Campbell, Teri Goetz, Elizabeth Hermon, Patty Lennon and Brooke Emery. These women have allowed me to map for them many times for many of their choices. They have read my book at different times. They have supported me through all of the emotional ups and downs that I have gone through in this decade. Debbie Teitelbaum has been my rock throughout this book and life.

My husband, Rich Pomerantz, has been patient, kind and willing to listen and read whenever I needed him. As a first reader, his thoughts and ideas encouraged me to take my writing to a deeper level. I am, however, most grateful for his calm reassurance and consolation in the moments that my inner critic spoke harshly.

My children, Tasha, Beck and Dane, were young teens when I began mapping and writing. The conversation of choice was infused into our household vocabulary and each, in their way, was receptive to navigating their choices with my new and expanding language. As they got older, they included their friends in the conversation, which was a blessing to me. The depth of the discussions I've had with them and their friends makes it abundantly clear to me that an important piece of my personal journey will be to coach and support the generations of emerging adults who are newly making their personal, professional and relationship choices.

My mother, Phyllis Martins, exhibited openness and vulnerability during her mapping experience which fostered us finding our way back to a deeply meaningful relationship.

Those Who Don't Know They Helped

Finally, I'd like to thank those who don't know they helped. At the beginning of this experience I could not fathom that I was a writer, let alone call myself one. I've since become a student of writing and I

Acknowledgements

want to thank Dani Shapiro, Linda Sivertsen, Gabby Bernstein, Julia Cameron and Brene Brown for the support and inspiration they've provided without realizing it.

About the Author

Kim DeYoung is a seasoned choice coach, entrepreneur and author with a passion for guiding individuals towards making meaningful choices. With over two decades of experience coaching visionary entrepreneurs, Kim has helped numerous people bring their ideas to life through intentional decision-making.

In her book, *The Book of Choice*, Kim offers a comprehensive guide to making intentional choices in all areas of life. By encouraging readers to ask thought-provoking questions and approach life with curiosity, she equips them with practical tools and insights to lead an examined life.

Before transitioning into choice coaching, Kim enjoyed a high-energy corporate career in the fashion industry, working with brilliant teams that fueled her drive for success. Later on, she discovered her love for entrepreneurship, particularly in guiding individuals to make purposeful choices in their personal and professional journeys.

Kim's workshops foster an encouraging environment that allows others to delve into their choices, gain valuable insights and navigate their way towards what truly matters to them. She also hosts the engaging podcast, *The Voice of Choice*, where she shares the transformative power of choice and interviews individuals who've made impactful decisions.

With her unique blend of expertise, compassion and positive energy, Kim is highly sought-after as a coach and speaker, inspiring individuals to make meaningful choices that create lasting impact.

To learn more about Kim, please visit http://kimdeyoung.com.

Online Resources

I've created a dedicated page with a collection of valuable resources, including templates for different types of maps, lists of questions to delve more deeply into your choices, and instructional videos on the map-making process.

Visit http://kimdeyoung.com/ChoiceResources to access these free tools and take your journey of exploration to the next level.

www.ingramcontent.com/pod-product-compliance
Lightning Source LLC
Chambersburg PA
CBHW071152130626
46553CB00004B/1631